CHRISTCHURCH HARBOUR

Michael Po'

Natula Publications

© Michael Powell 1995

ISBN 1 897 887 07 8

Natula Publications
Briar Park Business Centre
Stour Road
Christchurch
Dorset
BH23 1PL

British Library Cataloguing-In-Publication Data.
A catalogue record for this book is available from the British Library.

Printed by Southbourne Printing Company Ltd.
Seabourne Road, Bournemouth, Dorset, BH5 2HX

Dedication

To all those who, over the years, have contributed to making Christchurch Harbour the place it is today.

Cover Illustration

Christchurch Harbour Station on a weekday morning, sometime around 1905.

Had the plans of the Wimborne and Christchurch Railway come to fruition, giving the Somerset and Dorset Railway a cross-channel terminus, this scene might have become a reality. At the station pier the steamer 'Alberta', recently transferred from Southampton, awaits her midday departure. A boat train pulls out from the canopied platform behind her. In the foreground, a coastal paddle steamer departs for the Isle of Wight whilst 'Charlotte' is ahead of her in the main channel. The great arms of the twin, protective piers are hidden behind the eastern extremity of the headland. In the distance is Alum Bay on the Isle of Wight.

Illustration by Mark McIntyre, from an idea by the author

ACKNOWLEDGMENTS.

This work is the result of some twenty years, or so, of delving into the events which have occurred in and around the Christchurch Harbour. Much of the research commenced with material which was essentially anecdotal. A large number of people are associated with activities linked to the harbour. Many of them have known it for much of their lives, building up collections of documents and photographs which, by the nature of their approach, excel the contents of public archives. I have been privileged to have been allowed access to these and to have been provided with much additional material besides.

By their nature, acknowledgments are invidious. So many people have helped, knowingly or otherwise, in its compilation that a full list is simply not possible. I am grateful to everyone who has assisted me and in particular to Messrs. M. Hinton, R. Stride, J. and R. Elliott, M. Mannion, Mrs. J. Hawkins, Mr. and Mrs. Woodward and the late Messrs. K. Derham, H. Bemister and C. Keynes. In addition, I am indebted to the staffs of the Public Record Offices at Kew and Chancery Lane; the House of Lords' Record Office; the County Record Offices of Dorset, Hampshire and the Isle of Wight; Christchurch and Dorchester Libraries; the Red House Museum; Christchurch Borough Council and the Library and Archives of the Royal Engineers. Members of the Christchurch Local History Society and Christchurch Sailing Club have been very helpful in their advice and guidance. The help of Mr. M. Papworth, Regional Archaeologist for the National Trust (Wessex), who checked and offered advice concerning the earlier phases of the harbour's development, was invaluable.

I wish to record my gratitude to Bookends Bookshop of Church Street, Christchurch, who have made publication possible. Finally, (but certainly not least), I thank the members of my family for their help and support; my wife, Margaret, who has assisted with the research, who can also translate both Latin and my writing; Bryony, my daughter, who is developing an uncanny ability to find and note exactly the right information from headstones and my son, Alex, who can make a word-processor do things I am convinced it's not designed for. They have put up with a great deal to enable me to reach this stage.

Concentrating, as this book does, on commercial aspects and changes, both real and proposed, to the harbour, I consider this by way of an interim report. There is always more to find out. Whilst I have received unstinting support and advice, any errors or omissions remain my own.

Michael Powell, May 1995.

CONTENTS

Man before metal. The Neolithic Revolution. The Iron-age. The Roman Invasion and the conquest of the south-west. The Romano-British period.

The Saxon settlement. The beginnings of Christchurch. A royal manor. The Norman Conquest and the new order. Trade, fishing and ships 'for the King's purposes'.

The passage to Salisbury. Ship-money and blue-water sailors. Further plans. Smuggling and legal trade.

Plans for improvement. The commercial harbour of Christchurch. The Hengistbury Head Mining Company. The arrival of the railway and international proposals. Pleasure boats and excursions. Wrecks, close runs and the lifeboat. The twilight of trade.

The Great War. Pleasure boating. Further commercial activity. The Second World War. Ferries and bridges. Boat-building and fishing, the last harbour industries. The Mudeford lifeboat. Sailing and harbour amenities.

ILLUSTRATIONS

Chapter 5

Chapter 6

Introduction.

The harbour at Christchurch is formed by a broadening of the combined rivers Stour and Avon, forming an estuary on the last stage of their journey to the sea. A complex mixture of open water and marsh, the harbour is bounded to the south by the ironstone bulk of Hengistbury Head whilst, to the north, is the edge of the vast heath which contains the New Forest.

The rivers make their way to the sea through a narrow channel known as the Run, once a direct, straight entrance but whose form is now constantly changing. The Run is rather less than two hundred feet across and, at spring tides, the water flows through it at a rate in excess of five knots. The north-western side has been revetted and Mudeford Spit supports a quay for fishing craft and a ferry to the Hengistbury side. Behind these are a group of buildings including coastguard cottages, the Dutch House (formerly the 'Haven House' tavern, much used by smugglers two hundred years ago) and the latest 'Haven House'. The opposite side is a natural sandbank leading to an extensive sand spit which terminates in Hengistbury Head.

The approach to Christchurch Town through the harbour.

Just inside the entrance is a shoal, known as the Flats, which divides the channel, the northern arm spreading past Mudeford and its inshore lifeboat station, whilst the southern arm forms the main channel and the bed of the combined rivers. Varying in depth, but rarely exceeding six feet, the channel is flanked by sand and mud banks which dry out at low water radically changing the harbour's appearance. On Hengistbury sandbank stands the 'Black House' which once contained a boathouse and, next to it, is the site of a Nineteenth century shipyard. The sandbank is now largely covered with beach huts and their ancillary buildings and there is a jetty for the harbour's passenger service boats.

Between the channel and the flat marshland on Hengistbury's northern flank are lines of moorings and behind these is the entrance to a canal cut in the Nineteenth century to help with the extraction of ironstone. Just west of this are the remnants of limekilns, now known as the Knoll. The form of this shoreline has changed a great deal over the centuries; remains of pre-Roman harbour works have been discovered well back from the shoreline whilst much of the area of the contemporary settlement is now covered by Barn Bight. A channel immediately to the north of Hengistbury may represent an earlier course of the rivers. It is thought that, in prehistoric times, the rivers may have flowed into the sea to the west of Hengistbury, so changes to the harbour are not new.

Near the point where Barn Bight curves southwards, the channel turns north-west around the tail of Brander's Bank which divides the old and new river beds. On the northern side the harbour consists of numerous channels and creeks along the edge of Stanpit Marsh. Some of these extend nearly a mile inland and were a main reason for the place's popularity with smugglers. Mother Siller's channel (there are various spellings) can still be traced to the 'Ship in Distress' pub on the road from Christchurch to Mudeford. Near its entrance is Blackberry point, an island at high water.

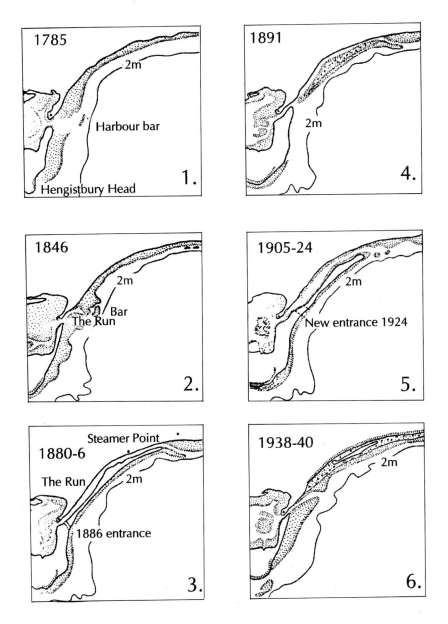

Alterations to the Run, 1785 - 1940.
(based on surveys in the possession of Christchurch Borough Council)
Since the removal of the ironstone, starting during the 1840s, coastal
erosion has greatly accelerated. The construction of the Long Groyne
has subsequently reduced it again, although creating new problems
further along the coast.

The main channel reverts to its westerly trend with Stanpit Marsh to the north and Brander's Bank to the south, across which the end of the Double Dykes is visible. The Double Dykes were the defences for the Hengistbury settlement during the Iron Age, the time of the harbour's international importance. West of these is the Marine Training Centre used by schools for water sport and safety training. It is also a centre for archaeological education.

Much of this shore is occupied by reed beds which were an important export source for generations up to this century. Beyond the head of Brander's Bank the harbour narrows between more reed beds and moorings begin again. Clay Pool marks the western limit of Stanpit Marsh and from here the water appears much more as a river than an open estuary. The Priory stands clearly a little way upstream, beyond the broad confluence of the rivers.

The Avon passes the northern side of the town in two channels forming an island, which was formerly common meadow, beneath two bridges and inland towards Ringwood and Salisbury. The southern arm flows close under the Priory, Castle and Constable's House. This was the site of the original town quay.

The Stour passes Christchurch Sailing Club, the present Town Quay and the mediaeval Place Mill. The mill stream is fed by, and runs parallel to, the Avon before emptying into the Stour. Quomps is a wide, open field bordered by a holiday camp opposite which is the village of Wick. There is a ferry at this point which has been operated more or less continuously since Saxon times. Bounded now by houses on the northern bank and public open space to the south, the river passes Tuckton with its passenger boat terminal and bridge. Beyond here is the former site of the Military Vehicles Experimental Establishment (one of the names used since it was Christchurch Barracks in the Eighteenth century) where the Bailey bridge was developed.

From the Run to the Town Quay at Christchurch is a distance of about a mile and a half. Compared to its harbour, the town is relatively young and, long before its foundation, the principal settlement was on the low-lying ground to the landward end of Hengistbury. Two thousand years ago, before the invasion of the Romans, this harbour was one of the principal ports of the known world.

Its position now, fifteen miles to the east of Poole and thirty west of Southampton - both major modern ports - makes it difficult to visualise Christchurch Harbour as anything more than a centre for sailing and fishing. Over the centuries it has served its communities well and has seen invasions, trade, storms, battles and, nearly, its own destruction. It has allowed the importing of the day-to-day goods which sustained the people of its shores through all the changes of history. 'It has been at the forefront of their attention for nearly all of the last two millennia, has been planned-for, developed, used and abused. It has survived all this and now, surrounded largely by accessible, open country, it forms a focus for recreational activity, simply the latest phase in a long and varied employment.

Chapter 1,
Early Days, Before Christchurch.

In what is now the United Kingdom, there is no contemporary written history prior to 55 BC, the year of the first Roman raid led by Julius Caesar. Archaeology is responsible for discovering, determining and interpreting everything before that date. Even after the commencement of documented history, archaeology has a major part to play as, particularly in the early stages, documentation is decidedly scanty and, even much later, fails to elucidate many of the details of day-to-day life which contemporary authors took for granted.

Archaeology endeavours to piece together the story of mankind's development by investigating the physical remains of his activities. Theories are developed on the basis of a corpus of discoveries. Later discoveries may either confirm such theories or require them to be reconsidered. What is acceptable as a hypothesis today may well be confounded by new discoveries tomorrow. The further back in time we go, the less information and, hence, the greater likelihood of gap-filling arguments being overturned. As more information becomes available, so theories may be built upon firmer foundations. This is by no means a new process. Two hundred years ago Voltaire wrote that "all our ancient history...is no more than accepted fiction".

Before the advent of man in his present, recognisable form, geology is the science which must be relied upon to provide evidence for and interpretation of change - change, by definition, outside the sphere of mankind's endeavour. Bearing in mind that there is much from the past which is either unknown or contentious, it is possible to piece together the early development, prehistory and then history of the harbour.

It is now generally believed that, immediately after the end of the last glaciation, the precursors of many of the various rivers which now empty into the sea between Poole and Chichester Harbour, fed a greater stream which flowed where the Solent is now. This combined river emptied between the present coasts of eastern Hampshire and the Isle of Wight, which was a peninsula joined to the mainland by a chalk ridge connecting with present day Purbeck. With the sea to the south, the valley behind this contained the streams which now flow east into Poole and empty there. North of this was a further ridge with another valley through which flowed the ancestor of the Stour, joined, well down-stream, by the proto-Avon. This river then combined with the streams in the southerly valley and together they flowed east to be met by the Test and other tributaries. The Solent and Spithead, off Portsmouth, are the sea-filled valleys of this distant time.

As sea levels rose after the ice retreated, so the English Channel spread eastward until it finally severed Britain from the European mainland. This event is now thought to have occurred between eight and ten-thousand years ago - a great deal more recent than was thought previously. As this was happening so pressure was being put on the chalk peninsula between Purbeck and the Isle of Wight and, at roughly the same time, it was breached. Rivers west of Southampton Water now had direct access to the sea and present-day geography becomes discernable. By this time, the influence of human beings was beginning to be felt.

It is usual to describe prehistory with titles relating to the principal tool-making material of the time. By this definition, we are still in the Iron-age. Once there is contemporary documentation (history), the titles relate to the most influential local peoples and, later, their leaders and monarchs. The earliest phase of humankind is the Stone-age. This is such an incomprehensibly long period, and contained so many developments, that it is divided into three major phases each of which is then sub-divided. The Palaeolithic is the earliest. Palaeolithic humanity had learnt the value of tools both of stone and organic materials. Over the hundreds of millennia, which this period occupied, these developed from simply using a handy rock to formed tools of great beauty as well as of specific use.

Man before metal.

The earliest current evidence for human activity on Hengistbury Head dates from the Upper Palaeolithic - the Old Stone-age - approximately twelve-thousand five hundred years ago. At this point in his development, man garnered what he could from his surroundings to supply his needs, making only the barest alterations to his environment. Essentially surviving by gathering and hunting their food, human beings lived a nomadic existence. They had knowledge of fire and could fashion sophisticated tools from stone, wood and bone. Of their language, beliefs and aspirations nothing will ever be known.

In 1913, flint tools of this period were discovered near the top of the vestige of a cove at the south-eastern corner of Hengistbury Head. These tools have been categorised to include weapon points, scrapers, knives and burins (including both chisels and tools for boring), which could have been used to manufacture other tools. The nature and scale of the finds may indicate that the site was used frequently over a lengthy period of time. At the time of their discovery, the site was referred to as the 'reindeer hunters' camp. It is now thought that horses may also have been their prey. Animals were hunted as much for their skin and bone as for their meat; it is probable that little of the kill was wasted after the expenditure of so much energy to bring it down. Similar complete use of hunted animals has been noted amongst nomadic peoples elsewhere in the world right into this century.

At the time that the camp was in use, Britain was still a peninsula of the European mainland and the Isle of Wight a peninsula to the south-east of Hengistbury, on each side of which flowed major rivers. The sea was several miles to the south. Things would remain this way, changing only gradually, for perhaps the next four and a half thousand years.

The next indications of activity on Hengistbury dates from three-thousand years later, around nine-thousand five hundred years ago. Britain may still not yet have become an island. The evidence is another camp site, this time from the Mesolithic or Middle Stone-age. The difference between the ages is largely one of technological ability, the development of tool types and the purposes to which they could be put. It is generally true that the nearer one comes to the present, the more specialised tools become. These people were also hunters but of different quarry. Deer and smaller creatures appear to have been their main targets. The tools found indicate a wider range of purpose and greater specialisation. Their method of manufacture was more sophisticated and the use of resin, as a glue, was understood. They possessed bows and arrows. Their camp may have been occupied for considerable periods of time together. There is evidence that food was stored against shortages or winter conditions. The site is now on the cliff edge about half-way between the earlier camp and the western end of Warren Hill.

These glimpses of man on Hengistbury are almost in the nature of a billowing curtain, disclosing a brief, barely observed scene before obscuring it again. During the four millennia before the next signs of human activity appear, some fundamental changes took place, not only in geography but in man's ability to amend his environment for his own benefit.

The Neolithic Revolution.

The union of what is now the English Channel and North Sea isolated Britain from continental developments until it became possible to build vessels capable of deep water voyages. The titles given to the developmental periods are in danger of becoming misleading the nearer modern times are approached. Many of the profound changes which humankind has undertaken, or undergone, were commenced in relative isolation in a number of different places, often as the result of chance discoveries. Others occurred singly and their influence spread like the proverbial ripples on a pond. This process takes time; the closer to the present, the briefer the dissemination period. This implies that the states of development of people in different parts of the world overlap. Even after the arrival or discovery of a new idea it was not necessarily taken up universally.

There is some evidence that sailing vessels existed in the Mediterranean before the time of Britain's isolation. There is no information concerning how long after this event it became possible to cross from the continent by boat. Bearing in mind that the French coast can be seen from the South Coast, and that the two coasts are not drawing closer together, it may well not have been very long. It is not a lack of technology which causes a problem, it is one of purpose. Very little is known of social or political organisation or trade (if any) at this period. It has been assumed that people lived in bands which were effectively self-sufficient and that the division from the mainland was of little developmental consequence.

How long the period of isolation lasted is a matter for conjecture. It is believed that around five and a half thousand years ago the last development of the Stone-ages began to infiltrate this island. So profound were the changes which it eventually spawned, that it is referred to by some as a revolution. It affected man's capacity to alter his environment, to begin the accelerating process in terms of materials, society and, eventually, politics which has led to his present status in perhaps one two-hundredth of the time it took to evolve through the earlier Stone-ages to the beginning of the Neolithic.

The Neolithic revolution began, in what is now referred to as the Middle East, around four to five thousand years before it reached the outer islands of present Europe. The principal change which it wrought was concerned with the acquisition of food. Throughout his earlier development, mankind had been dependent on what he could find and catch. In the Neolithic he began to produce his own. By growing staple crops and herding animals, human beings were freed from one of life's major problems. This is not to argue that gathering, fishing and hunting were immediately outmoded - they continue to this day - but rather that time could now be given to other pursuits and considerations.

These fundamental changes brought about conditions where

settled life became possible. The concept of permanent villages was an early step towards the bases of civilisation. Specialisation of skills and the availability of time may have been key factors in this process of change which was developing in Britain at about the same time that the Sumerians were recording the results of using standard measures and the Sphinx and Khufu's pyramid were already gracing the Egyptian landscape.

Well into this period, there was a settlement at Hengistbury, which was by now a coastal feature. Excavation has revealed large quantities of both stone tools and pottery, although no evidence of structures. Worked flakes have also been found on the northern side of the harbour. The presence of pottery indicates a need for long-term storage which, in turn, implies a relatively settled existence. The tools available in the Neolithic were quite capable of clearing woodland preparatory to cultivation and new types, such as sickles, indicate harvesting. Tools have been found - delicate, leaf shaped blades - whose only purpose can have been the demonstration of skill. These people buried their dead in long barrows, indicating belief in an afterlife; fished from skin-covered boats; wove textiles and, sometimes, grew enough produce to create a surplus. This could be exchanged for the different produce of others - the beginnings of trade. Trackways began to link settlements and along these travelled the specialist produce of each region.

It appears that the Hengistbury Neolithic settlement was in use around four thousand years ago but for how long, or why it was abandoned, is unknown. There then followed a long period during which there is no direct evidence for settlement on Hengistbury although a number of round barrows, the burial mounds of a later people, indicate its use as a cemetery. These people arrived about five hundred years after the supposed Neolithic abandonment and possessed a radically new material, one which required a high level of technology for its manufacture - bronze. As with earlier 'new ages', bronze did not supersede stone completely or even to any great extent. It was expensive to produce but nevertheless represents the first large scale use of metal. New tools and weapons became possible - such as swords - impossible to make from flint.

There is some indication that agriculture in this area gave way to a pastoral, semi-nomadic lifestyle to some extent during the Bronze age, which may account for the absence of settlement evidence on the headland. This era saw the completion of Stonehenge on Salisbury Plain, then one of the most heavily populated regions in the island. Finds of grave goods show that there were trading links at this time with places as far away as Egypt and Scandinavia as well as the European mainland and Ireland. As the two main rivers from the plain flow into the sea at Christchurch, it is possible that they were imported through the harbour.

A further gap in the Hengistbury record now occurs, terminating less than three thousand years ago with the appearance of a new group with a new material. Iron is more readily available, easier to produce and has a wider range of applications than bronze and a large proportion of Hengistbury Head consists of its ore.

The Iron-age.

The technology for working iron was brought to Britain by the Celts. Celtic settlement around Christchurch Harbour appears to have taken place in two distinct phases. The earlier of these began around 600 BC (although the earliest use of iron may date from around two hundred years earlier). Mingling with, or perhaps to some extent displacing, the earlier occupants, there are a number of Iron-age sites along the valley of the Stour in the immediate area. The principal of these was at Hengistbury. The Head provided vast quantities of iron ore and was in close proximity with land suitable for agriculture. The headland sheltered the harbour from the prevailing winds and the rivers provided both hunting for wildfowl and a means of access into the interior. There was a settlement here which has revealed traces of industry in the form of metal workers' hearths, scrap material and imported, hand-formed pottery. Domestic sites indicate that these people lived in round, thatched, wattle-and-daub huts. To differentiate it from later periods, this culture is sometimes referred to as Iron-age A.

After a period of about two hundred years the site declined in importance and may have been abandoned again. Why this was so is uncertain but it may indicate economic or political pressure. This was by no means the last use of Hengistbury, or its harbour, by the Celts. The final period represents, perhaps, its golden age.

Archaeological Excavations, Hengistbury Settlement Site.

Around 100 BC a new settlement appeared at Hengistbury. The Celts, highly organised and warlike people, looked upon their tribe as their people and various tribes occupied virtually the whole country. The tribe, whose area included Hengistbury, was the Durotriges, from whose name both Dorset and Dorchester are partly derived. These were the people who brought the hill-forts to their final form, possibly as administrative centres for their immediate districts. They had developed sophisticated trading and political links with their neighbours both in Britain and on the Continent.

The value of Hengistbury as a port at this period lay, not only in its sheltered position and easily recognisable profile when searching for a landfall, but also in its proximity with the Cotentin peninsula jutting north from the coast of France. This area was occupied by the Veneti whose way of life reflected the Durotriges and who also had economic links with the growing area of Roman influence.

The culture of the Celts had developed to a point where trade had acquired a pivotal importance. By the first century BC tribes east of the Avon had begun to resite settlements away from the hill-forts to places which were more suitable for the practice of trade. In international terms Hengistbury was to become the supreme example. For trade to develop, a number of circumstances must exist. The population must be fairly settled and living at a level above that of mere subsistence. There needs to be a surplus of produce or specialised products not easily obtainable by, and desirable to, trading partners and there must be transport technology available. At this time all this was in place.

Double Dykes - the Iron-age defences of Hengistbury Head.

The peninsula had acquired its defences - the Double Dykes - which provided protection from landward. As a promontory fort it was strikingly similar to those of the Veneti. Within the ramparts there was land enough for a large settlement, rudimentary port facilities and agriculture. The present entrances through the dykes are relatively modern. The original entrance is close to the end nearest the harbour. It comprised a causeway across the intervening ditch defended by hornworks and including a barbican between, and overlooked by, the ramparts. The line of the defences, which are largely north to south across the neck of the promontory, bear east at this point and so, once inside, people entering by the gate would pass down a ramp overlooked by the ramparts for much of its distance. The inner rampart would have possessed a timber-faced palisade and wall walk. The outer may also have been similarly equipped. The concept of these defences was to prevent capture by storm and to place defenders outside the range of projectile weapons whilst allowing return fire to find targets. The weapons concerned were the spear and the slingshot. Against these they were spectacularly effective. There is little evidence for the capture of any hill-forts by these methods during the Iron-age.

At this time the reed beds were not so advanced and Barn Bight cut in less deeply. The main settlement area was on the shore of the bight, extending along it and inland for a considerable distance. As well as domestic accommodation, a number of industries were carried on. Amongst the materials imported into the site were lead from the Mendips, copper and silver-bearing copper ore from the south-west, shale from Kimmeridge, glass blocks from the continent and scrap gold from inland. Much of this material seems to have been worked on the site and some, particularly the extraction of silver from argentiforous copper, requires substantial, permanent industrial facilities. The silver may have been re-exported as ingots or coinage. There may have been a mint at the settlement. At the same time the community was effectively self-sufficient in terms of iron ore, food and daily requirements.

Much of the trade would have passed along the valley of the

Stour and, to a lesser extent, the Avon. The course of the Avon was less well-defined and its flood-plain was marshier and less easily traversed. Trade to the continent required sea-going ships and suitable port facilities. Although there is no archaeological evidence for the type of vessels in use at the time, Caesar provides a description of those of the Veneti with whom he had to fight. Very different from the ships he was used to, Caesar describes them as relatively flat-bottomed to ride in shoal water and to take the ground. They were built of oak with high stems and sterns 'for use in heavy seas and violent gales', had beams a foot wide held by iron bolts and anchors fitted with chain cable. The sails were of leather and they carried no oars. The Veneti were the most powerful tribe on that coast, possessed the largest fleet and controlled all the few harbours. These were probably the kind of ships which traded to Hengistbury. A Venetic pattern anchor, together with part of its chain cable, has been recovered from a site near Poole.

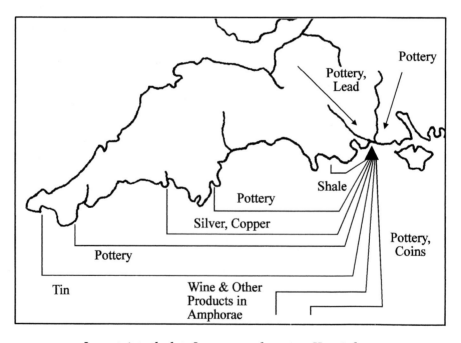

Imports into the late Iron-age settlement at Hengistbury.

Amongst the finds from the later Iron-age site are numbers of shards of amphorae. The amphora was, in effect, the standard means of packaging anything that could be treated as a fluid in the classical world. Their origins can often be distinguished by shape. Many of the Hengistbury finds originated in Italy and once contained wine. There is a suggestion that this trade was relatively direct. The Roman writer Strabo lists some of the exports at the time including corn, cattle, iron, slaves, hides and hunting dogs. He attributes the Venetis' defiance of Caesar to not wanting him to invade Britain and spoil their lucrative trading links. Strabo points out that the tribe was using the trading centre there. He may very well be referring to Hengistbury. Pliny mentions tin which may have been transferred by coaster from the area of Mounts Bay to Hengistbury and hence across the Channel. Other writers mention an export trade in chariots which, in Britain, were built mainly of wicker. Long outmoded as a means of warfare in the classical world, they were still popular for racing, and British chariots were very light.

The port facilities to support this trade may have been rudimentary. Right until the present day some coastal trading ships take the ground for off-loading. This may have been the practice then. Some evidence for the port has been found. It consists principally of deliberately built-up gravel beaches discovered a little to the east of the settlement site. This site is now a little way inland because of changes to the configuration of the shore line. Although there is no indication of a quay, some such may have existed.

In spite of the efforts of the Veneti, Caesar did raid Britain - twice - in 55 and 54 BC. These were not permanent invasions but led to agreements for tribute and military aid on the part of some tribes. These events, combined with increasing Roman influence, and later control, across the Channel, led to a decline in the harbour's status. The community continued to survive and Hengistbury probably remained one of the principal Durotrigian settlements. New trade routes from the Channel's southern coast to the heart of the Empire were encouraged via the rivers Seine and Rhine. This moved the focus of the remaining trade to the east and began the pattern which largely survives today - the short sea-crossing via the Dover Strait. Hengistbury continued in use as a local centre and may even have retained its mint. Nearly a century after Caesar's raids an event occurred which was eventually to put paid to native ways forever.

In 43 AD, basing his justification partly on the agreements of Caesar's day, the emperor Claudius undertook the invasion and permanent annexation of Britain to the empire of Rome.

The Roman invasion and conquest of the south-west.

The invasion force consisted of four legions, drawn from the Rhine frontier, together with auxiliary units, and numbered around forty thousand troops. The landings took place near modern Dover and the North Foreland, the groups combining near the site of Canterbury, fighting across the Medway and then the Thames to enter the tribal territory of the Catuvelauni. The tribe's surrender to Claudius himself marked the end of the first phase.

It is probable that the tribes of the south-west spent much of that year refurbishing their fortifications. Late, and sometimes incomplete, additional banks at forts such as Badbury may indicate a hasty response to news of Rome's fighting techniques and weapons. The army of Rome was a professional organisation. Soldiers joined expecting to serve their time and then retire with a gratuity and a grant of land. Their fighting methods were designed to destroy the enemy at minimum risk to themselves. Each legion, containing around five thousand men, possessed a number of long-range weapons and siege engines which they would put to good effect during the campaign in the south-west.

The Second Legion (Augusta), under the command of Titus Flavius Vespasianus, was despatched, probably in the following year, to friendly territory near Chichester where they set up a base. Making full use of the naval forces available to them, the Second Augusta annexed the country as far west as Exeter over the following four years. The Roman historian, Tacitus, describes how the legion captured Vectis (the Isle of Wight) by force and then went on to capture twenty 'oppida', fortified towns or hill-forts, during the course of the campaign. Maiden Castle, near Dorchester, Spetisbury Rings and Hod Hill (both on the Stour) were amongst these. Badbury may also have been as there is evidence of a temporary legionary fortress at Lake Farm near Wimborne and a fort for a smaller unit at Crab Farm, just south of the Rings.

Ring Intaglio from Waddon Hill. It shows Augustus' badge, the capricorn, together with the prow of a galley.

Supplies and equipment for this phase may have been brought in through Hamworthy, in Poole Harbour, the terminus of one of the Roman roads which cross near Badbury. There is visible evidence of Roman fortifications at Hod Hill where a unit was based to police the area after the main force had moved on. Waddon Hill, near Beaminster, revealed a ring intaglio showing the prow of a galley beneath the capricorn emblem of the Second Augusta. It has been suggested that it may have been the property of a marine officer.

There is no evidence of additional construction at Hengistbury but it may be assumed that vessels attached to Vespasian's legion reconnoitred it. It may be that their trade links made the people of the area more aware than most of the power of Rome and that, therefore, they put up no fight. They may have hoped for a return to international status in the face of the inevitable trading shift towards the Dover Strait. The new administration preferred the ports of Hamworthy and Clausentum (Bitterne, near Southampton) to Christchurch and the settlement declined.

The Romano-British period.

It may be that some of the territory of the Durotriges was turned over to estates administered on behalf of the Emperor for the remainder of the First century. Later the tribe was given its own administration, centred on Durnovaria (Dorchester). The road from Isca (Exeter) to Londinium (London) ran through it, turning north-east to pass Vindocladia (close to Badbury) and leaving the area of the Avon and Lower Stour valleys as something of a backwater. Hengistbury became an agricultural settlement and may have served to export some of the local produce. The type of ship used may have been similar to the Romano-British coaster excavated near Blackfriars Bridge, London, during the 1970s. Heavily constructed, it owed more to Celtic than Roman design. The remains of a supposed Roman ship were discovered in the Harbour around 1912 but have, regrettably, been lost.

During Boudicca's rising in the 60s, some of the Durotriges further west sympathised with her cause. The legion which had taken the area moved on from Exeter to Gloucester and, later, to Caerleon in Wales. There they were based for around three hundred years until they were moved, in divisions, to man the Forts of the Saxon Shore along the south-east coast. Their commander during the invasion went on to become Emperor.

Hengistbury retained its agricultural status throughout the period, which lasted for nearly four hundred years, despite the occasional political upheaval. The road system linking the new towns passed it by and so did the new pattern of trade. Towards the end of this time, as the danger from Saxon raids increased, it may have been re-occupied on a more substantial basis. The Durotriges, having been so poorly treated in the early phase of the invasion, eventually became amongst the most loyal of the Romano-British.

In 409AD the remaining forces were recalled to the Continent to resist pressures on the heart of the Empire. In this they ultimately failed. It may be that a small contingent, perhaps in the role of advisors, returned for a few years from about 417 but, after that, the islanders were left to make the best efforts they could in retaining the civilisation they had embraced. Midway along the south coast, Hengistbury may have become a target for the next phase of invaders.

Chapter 2,
The Middle Ages and the Founding of Christchurch.

There is very little evidence concerning events in the area of the harbour during the sub-Roman period. In much of the central-southern region, the hill-forts were reactivated and the cities gradually abandoned as they became targets for the latest wave of raiders. As central administration broke down, and mercenaries were employed to protect the interests of those left in charge by the Romans, so anarchy reigned in some places, the vestiges of order in others.

Legend names Hengistbury as the landing place of the Saxon leader Hengist. He and his comrade-in-arms Horsa were employed by the Kentish leader, Vortigern (the word is a title rather than a name), to aid in the defence of the eastern coast against other Saxons. This is one factor which makes the legend less than likely. Another is the earthen Bockerly Dyke near the present border of Dorset and Wiltshire. This was constructed originally during the late 4th century at a time when troops had been temporarily withdrawn. It cut the road from London to the south-west. This was reconstructed before the beginning of the 5th century, then the dyke re-erected after 410. The Durotriges tried hard to retain their Romanisation and were successful for longer than elsewhere in what soon became Wessex. The tide of the Saxon settlement largely flowed round them.

Some believe that the legendary 'king' Arthur (Arta means bear in the Celtic language, Ursa means the same in Latin - a battle-name for an unknown leader who was certainly real) fought the battle of Badon at Badbury, near Wimborne. Although there are other contenders for this honour, it is in the right place, geographically, and the Durotrigian attitude increases the possibility. The battle held off further incursions for a generation.

The Saxon settlement.

As well as the overland sweep of the Saxons, small groups

settled on likely inlets and estuaries as landing places. Around 530 AD, the Saxon leader, Cerdic, captured the Isle of Wight and advanced north along the river valleys to join with the Hwiccas in the Thames valley. It was not, though, an organised military invasion in the way that the Romans' had been. Christchurch would seem a likely target for such activity. It is possible that the first settlement on the present site dates from this period.

Christianity, the state religion for the last eighty years of Roman rule, retreated westward in the face of these incursions. Remote from the continent, it developed its own traditions which set it apart from the mainstream of Catholicism. During the two centuries which followed the termination of direct Roman rule the country came, eventually, to be divided into a varying number of kingdoms. This area became part of Wessex, the Kingdom of the West Saxons.

The beginnings of Christchurch.

The divisions between the two streams of the church became apparent after Augustine's arrival at the court of Ethelbert of Kent. They were settled at the Synod of Whitby, sixty-seven years later, giving ascendancy to the Roman church and, with it, the beginnings of the new pattern of monasteries. The date for the establishment of the monastery at Twynham is uncertain. The first ecclesiastical foundation was Celtic in origin and amongst the various legends which abound, the most likely is that ascribing it to Oswald, King of Northumbria around the end of the 630s. The purpose of the church, dedicated to the Holy Trinity, was to provide a base for missionary work in the remote country around the harbour and its neighbouring heathland.

As the years progressed a town developed close to the monastery, to serve the needs of its visitors and those who brought its produce from the lands it came to acquire on the Isle of Wight. The site was ideal, set on a gravel bank at the confluence of two major rivers (the early name Twynham is derived from Tweoxneam meaning 'between the waters'), served by a secure natural harbour yet still a safe distance from the open sea. This was soon to become important as Saxon England began to fall prey to the next wave of marauders - the Vikings.

A royal manor.

The first Norse attack on England occurred in 789 AD near the present site of Weymouth and amongst its first victims was the King's Reeve from Dorchester who had travelled down to meet what he probably thought was a trading party. There then followed nearly eighty years during which the Viking foothold became an annexation of nearly half the area of modern England, centred mainly on York. Constant intrusions into the south were held off with no surety of long-lasting success until the accession of Alfred (known as 'The Great') in 871 AD.

At around this time the settlement of Christchurch and its surrounding hinterland became a royal manor. Alfred established a system of fortified strongholds to defend land, population and trade. Twynham was one of these. At Alfred's death in 901 AD the succession of his son, Edward, was challenged by a cousin, Ethelwald, who seized both the fortified settlements of Wimborne and Twynham. Edward moved against him, camping at Badbury preparatory to attacking Wimborne. Ethelwald fled in the night, eventually fetching up in Northumbria. At what stage, precisely, Twynham became fortified is uncertain as is its exact form. The remains of the town wall of this period are still visible in part as a low bank in Druitt Gardens.

Druitt Gardens - probable remains of part of the Saxon wall.

A generation later, during the reign of Athelstan, a further reorganisation of the burghal system took place. This involved the relocation of some of the burghs to places more suitable as trading centres rather than simply local defences. Twynham escaped being effectively closed down only because, being on a royal manor, its revenues went direct to the King.

In 990 AD Ethelred the Redeless ordered all seaworthy ships, including those of Twynham, to assemble for an attack on the latest Viking fleet following a decade of destruction which included the burning of Southampton. There was no battle and Ethelred resorted to paying off the attackers. In Alfred's day, a fleet such as this had been destroyed off Purbeck by a combination of Saxon zeal and the weather. Such times were now gone. Ethelred was succeeded by a Norse king.

The Norman Conquest and the new order.

The Saxon line came to a final end on the battlefield of Senlac on October 14th, 1066. William, Duke of Normandy, succeeded Harold of Wessex by conquest and was crowned king at both Winchester - the old capital of Wessex - and London. He instituted a new approach to administration which led to profound changes, not least in Twynham.

Although retaining technical ownership of all land, William distributed vast tracts of it to loyal followers and the church. They, in turn, distributed much of their holdings to equally loyal supporters. Except for the church, the payment for this privilege was by military service as required within agreed limits. This way William had his land controlled and an army available when needed. To a lesser extent, this also applied to the great landholders and so their holdings were split up geographically. Should they collect their forces together, the King would be aware of it.

As it had been a royal manor before the Conquest, William held Twynham himself until 1100. In that year he passed it to Richard de Redvers who added it to his holdings near Exeter and on the Isle of Wight. The first castle was a timber 'motte and bailey' construction, refurbished in stone within a few years. The material for this work was brought in by sea and off-loaded at a point on the modern Convent Walk known as the 'Works'. It is possible that this name stems from that time for the stone, for the later Constable's House (built to replace uncomfortable accommodation in the keep) and Priory, was also landed here. Later it was the site of the town quay.

The construction of the castle provided an opportunity to display power for its own sake. All the buildings along the street leading to the bridge over the Avon were demolished to make room for the castle ditch. Castle Street now makes a displaced crossroads in the town centre. There was no better reason for this than to show that it could be done. The castle itself was built principally to control and overawe the town rather than to defend it.

A new site was proposed for the church, at St. Catherine's Hill, about two miles from the old buildings. Legend has it that the materials were constantly removed to the original site each night until the decision was changed and the new church went up on the site of the old. The domestic buildings were probably left until last for reconstruction. Nearly all the timber and all of the stone would have been transferred to the quay by sea. In 1150, Canons Regular of the Order of St. Augustine were installed in what now became the Priory, a reduction in the number of the earlier order having been engineered from two dozen to five. Further work ensued on the church and conventual buildings which continued on and off for a further four and a half centuries. The necessary material, including stone from France, Purbeck and the Isle of Wight, came by ship through the harbour to the 'Works'. To this traffic was added the produce of the Priory's lands on the Isle of Wight.

Trade, fishing and ships 'for the King's purposes'.

A large proportion of Twynham's economy in Saxon times must have been based on fishing. By the time of the Conquest, the monastery possessed fishery rights in the estuary of the two rivers. They had the rights to all fish caught in the harbour except salmon. In 1150 they were granted rights to one salmon per year which was quickly upgraded to ten per cent of the catch. The monastery also owned fisheries at Gloucester (dating from 905 AD) and Glastonbury (954 AD). The Royalty fishery was established around the beginning of the Thirteenth century. Some oyster fishing was also carried out, initially for the church but later for general sale. There is some evidence of salt extraction on the north shore of Hengistbury Head and it has been suggested that tidal fish-ponds existed nearby.

The coastal sea routes were the preferred means of transporting goods and produce whenever possible at this time. No properly constructed roads had been built since the Roman occupation, now nearly a thousand years earlier. What tracks there were suffered more from impassability than other dangers. This situation lasted until the turnpikes began to be built in the Eighteenth century. Being the harbour for a town of major local importance, Christchurch possessed ships of its own both for trading and fishing, although it was considered an out-port, or creek, of Southampton from the time of the conquest. Consequently it was liable to provide ships for the King's purposes as required.

The first recorded instance is in 1206, during the reign of King John. The Constable of Southampton ordered Christchurch to provide all vessels capable of carrying eight or more horses to assemble for an expedition to recapture lost areas of France. In 1302, Edward 1 was preparing an attempt to gain permanent control of Scotland and amongst his ships was one provided by the Priory.

There is some evidence for peaceful trading as well, although it comes from later in the period. Amongst the dockets for the payment of duty are those for a cargo of teazels (used for carding wool) registered to the ship's master, John William, during 1427. On the last day of October, 1439, a Christchurch ship left Southampton under the command of John Molam, with a cargo of two bales of alum and two barrels of white soap for William Duke of Exeter. On

February 22nd of the following year, the same ship and commander was carrying two pipes of wine registered to the master.

There may have been some water-borne trade down the Avon at this time. Salisbury had supplied a ship, the *'Trout'*, for Henry VI's service in defending the Kent coast in 1440 and, a little later, a syndicate of Salisbury merchants owned the *'Antelope'* of Poole. In 1535 Henry VIII ordered the removal of all fish weirs from the Avon as they impeded navigation.

The modern era is considered by some to commence with the Renaissance. In Britain it is common to date it from 1485, the year of the battle of Bosworth which ended the Wars of the Roses. Henry VII, the victor, set about dismantling the remnants of the feudal system, which had been introduced by the Normans, and reducing the power of the surviving nobility.

As far as Christchurch was concerned its trade had reached a point where active improvement to its facilities were about to be proposed and a long cycle of change and development to commence.

Southampton   Lyme Regis   Melcombe Regis

Town seals from the Middle-ages.

Chapter 3,
Improvements, Ship Money & Smuggling.

The passage to Salisbury.

The cathedral city of Salisbury stands at the southern edge of the chalk upland plain of the same name, which occupies much of central Wiltshire. In Roman times it was known as Soriodunum and replaced the hill-fort settlement now known as Old Sarum. It is some twenty miles north of Christchurch to which it is connected by the River Avon, its nearest access to the sea. In the Middle Ages, much of Salisbury's wealth was dependent on wool which was shipped out through Southampton. This was the predominant route for its trade.

From time to time, though, between the Fifteenth and Eighteenth centuries, attempts were made to open a permanent, direct link with Christchurch. Apart from Southampton, Salisbury merchants had interests in other ports. The *'Trout'* and *'Antelope'* have already been mentioned, as has Henry VIII's directive to remove the fish weirs from the Avon.

The village of Downton is some four miles south of Salisbury. The Lord of the Manor in 1586 was Sir Walter Raleigh. In that year he experienced a sudden, pressing need to expand his house there in expectation of an impending visit from Queen Elizabeth. Royal travel in those days involved the movement of dozens, if not hundreds, of people to defend and see to the needs of the monarch. To provide the timber for the work, Raleigh acquired the hulk of an old merchant ship which was towed up the river to Downton, broken up near the site and its frames and beams re-used. The timbers today support part of the roof of Downton Manor House. The salt-saturated wood shows no sign of deterioration.

The implication that the river was navigable in certain seasons is supported by the journey, some thirty-nine years later, of John Taylor. Taylor was a London wherryman and poet at a time when the Thames was one of the capital's principal highways. In 1625, using a wherry - a large, shallow draught boat which was designed for rowing but could also carry a sail - he enjoyed an eventful voyage from Christchurch to Salisbury. Met by civic dignitaries at each landing, some escorted by trumpeters to sound fanfares, Taylor established that the river could be used and gained much support for the concept.

Although there was no immediate commencement, the idea persisted. In 1655, during the Commonwealth period, representations were made to Cromwell by Francis Mathew to provide for the opening of the Avon to navigation from Christchurch. This was intended for the use of '..small, flat-bottomed vessels, bilanders of 30 tons which, laden, draw only three foot water: and this as well for the sea, and its commodities to be imported...'. Although, once again, no action was taken, the idea began to acquire some powerful friends. Following the restoration in 1660, the Earl of Clarendon began pressuring for the concept to be reconsidered. The owner of much land in the area, Clarendon saw the potential commercial possibilities. In 1664 he became the chief commissioner of the project under the terms of 'The River Avon Navigation Act'. This allowed for any necessary harbour or river improvements to be carried out. Once again there was no immediate rush, though land alongside the Stour was given to Christchurch by Viscount Cornbury for the purposes of constructing a new town quay.

Clarendon's Rocks ,visible at low water, are a hazard to boats.

Clarendon's scheme of 1671.

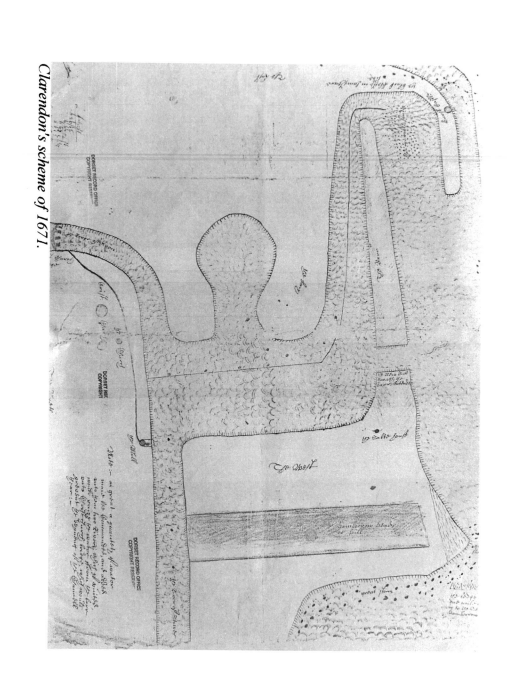

In 1668, following the fiasco of the Second Dutch War, Clarendon fell from power and went into exile from which he never returned. Virtually continuous wars had increased awareness of the value of a strong navy and the dormant plans for Christchurch were given a necessary boost by the publication, in 1677, of Andrew Yarranton's ' England's Improvement by Sea and Land'. Yarranton, who claimed to have surveyed the entire coasts of England, Wales and Ireland, enthused about the naval and defensive possibilities of Christchurch.

Rightly claiming that the sheltered harbour was ideally situated to defend the approaches to Southampton, he noted that the proximity of the forest would provide easy access to ship-building timber. The ironstone of Hengistbury would provide a source of the material for guns and ships' fittings and these could be made at Ringwood, the river being used as the linking route. The problem of the harbour's shallow depth was ignored, perhaps Yarranton made his 'survey' at high water.

By this time the river was useable as, only eight years after the passing of the Act, Bishop Ward of Salisbury had personally provided funds to finish the work on that part of the scheme. Two years later, in 1674, the minutes of Sarum Corporation record the arrival at Crane Bridge of two ships from Christchurch bearing twenty-five tons of cargo.

Britford Lock.

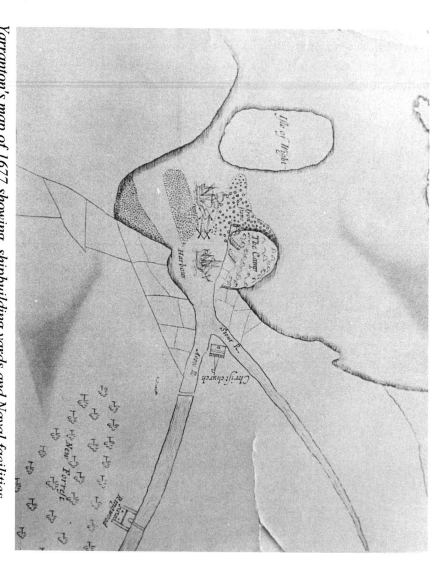

Yarranton's map of 1677 showing shipbuilding yards and Naval facilities.

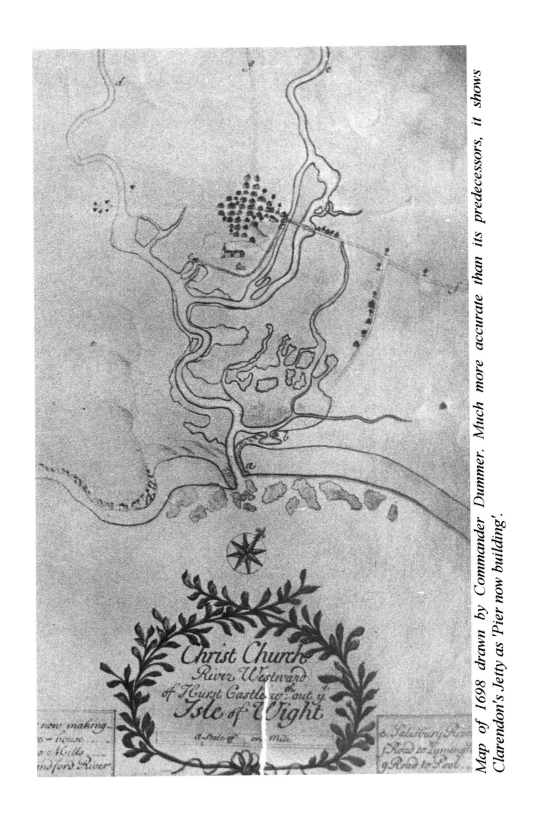

Map of 1698 drawn by Commander Dummer. Much more accurate than its predecessors, it shows Clarendon's Jetty as 'Pier now building'.

Back at the harbour, a proper survey was carried out in 1692 and work finally put in hand on a new entrance and protective jetty. All this effort was to be rapidly undone. On Friday, November 26th, 1703, there began a storm which is generally considered to have been the most savage until the hurricane of 1987. The damage it caused included the wrecking of over three hundred ships, the destruction of hundreds of buildings and thousands of trees. It also sealed the new harbour entrance at Christchurch, after less than a decade's use. The evidence of witnesses at a hearing concerning fishing rights on the Avon in Wiltshire in 1737, to the effect that ships were constantly using the river and had been doing so 'since time out of mind', was probably wishful thinking. As late as 1771, James Brindley, the canal engineer, recommended a new cut parallel with the whole length of the river. It was deemed too expensive a project and the navigation was formally closed to commerce during the following year. Although long drawn-out and ultimately short-lived, this was only the first of many proposals over the years to improve the facilities of Christchurch Harbour.

Ship-money and blue-water traders.

One of the much-quoted reasons for the rift between Charles 1st and Parliament is the issue of Ship-money. This was a tax raised by the King without Parliament's consent being necessary. Its purpose was to provide warships to defend the coast from both unfriendly foreign powers and pirates. Christchurch paid its quota up until 1639, three years before the Civil War broke out. Ship money had replaced the earlier practice of supplying the actual ships, as the monarch required. Warships were, by now, specialised and could no longer be temporarily converted from merchantmen.

Whilst piracy along the coast of southern England seems unlikely, there are a number of well-attested incidents affecting Christchurch. Some of these pirates came from as far away as north Africa - Barbary Corsairs. In 1626, the Corporation made a payment of twelve shillings for the relief of '...poor travellers taken by the Turks...' and in 1631 one shilling was provided for seven men taken by pirates from Dunkirk. Ship-money, properly spent, was not an unnecessary tax.

Although trade into Christchurch was purely coastal, there is evidence of sailors from the town serving in deep-water trades. In 1638, William Butcher, of Christchurch, was serving as a seaman in the ship 'Phoenix' of Southampton. On a voyage from Tenerife in the Canary Islands, part of the cargo of wine was destroyed and his name appears on the list of deponents to the subsequent enquiry.

Further plans

In 1745, amongst much discussion of the merits of improving Dover and Deal for the burgeoning cross-channel trade, a correspondent signing himself 'E.S.', writing in the 'Gentleman's Magazine', proposed the development of Christchurch Harbour as an alternative. Although nothing more was heard of this scheme, in 1762 the Corporation employed John Smeaton to survey the harbour and recommend action for making it a deep water port. Smeaton had made his name as a mill engineer and had recently diversified into other structures. His best known work is probably the Eddystone lighthouse near Plymouth. His was the third structure to be erected on the rock and the first to be able to adequately withstand the weather. Now replaced by the fourth Eddystone light, his tower was re-built on Plymouth Hoe, where it still stands.

Smeaton evaluated the problem of sand banks building up in the harbour and its entrance, ascribing it to the relatively small tidal range and the proximity of the Isle of Wight, which produced the double high water effect. He concluded that the only reason that the harbour had not already become silted-up was the strength of the current of the combined rivers flowing through it. He was dubious that the harbour could ever be developed to a point where it could handle deep-water vessels but, nevertheless, offered a number of recommendations for improvement. He suggested the construction of a new, five-hundred foot pier, parallel to, and to the south of, Clarendon's jetty, to accelerate the flow and cause the rivers to deposit

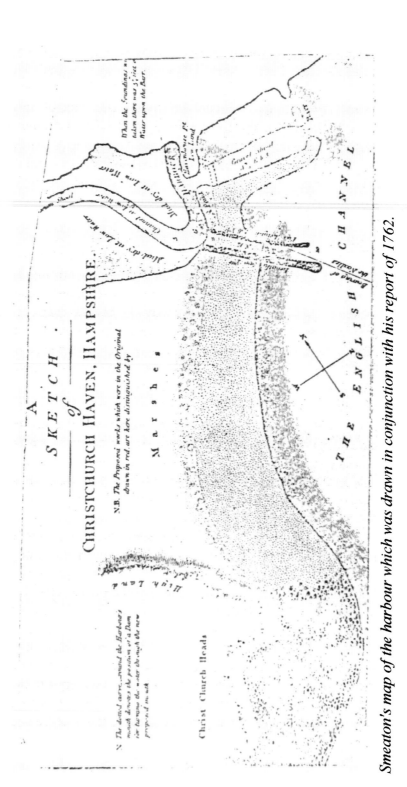

Smeaton's map of the harbour which was drawn in conjunction with his report of 1762.

their suspended sand and mud beyond the harbour bar. The existing, natural entrance would be closed. The pier would be built mainly from ironstone with Portland stone being used when the material from Hengistbury ran out. Although he noted the erosion already happening, he failed to comment on the possible effects of removing the protective ironstone from the foreshore of the Head. Smeaton estimated the cost at £5,000. The scheme was shelved.

Smuggling and legal trade.

Although it possessed some regional importance by the middle of the Eighteenth century, Christchurch was still relatively remote from its neighbours, separated from them by heathland and forest. With its own harbour it was, to some extent, self-sufficient and trade developed as required to serve the needs of its population, then numbering around two thousand. Its remoteness led to its central place in the great, illegitimate trade which developed throughout the century until it threatened to outstrip legal trade and starve the government of revenue.

Smuggling on this scale was brought about by a number of factors. There was little romance in the reality of 'free trading'. A combination of extreme poverty, greed and poorly conceived taxation created the opportunity for its existence, whilst personal gain and a misconception that it was a victim-less crime allowed it to continue. The attitude that the practice hurt no-one permeated right through society. Smuggling was highly organised, often with otherwise respectable businessmen putting up the funds. The importing was carried out using ships sometimes specially built for the trade, often manned by local fishermen. Once landed, labourers and farmers were recruited to help with distribution.

Against a widespread activity which might involve any member of the community, the authorities established the 'preventative service', both the Boards of Customs and of Excise having their own officers, patrols and coast-watching fleets. Each could call for assistance from military or naval forces - assuming they were available. Some of the services' personnel worked long and hard in an unpopular task to try to reduce the problem. Many saw an opportunity for profit and took their cut.

There are numerous stories concerning smuggling along this coast and some of them are true. A majority, however, contain more myth than reality. Even those with a basis in fact usually revert to the approach that smugglers were involved in a game with overbearing authority and, therefore, deserved to win. In the Eighteenth century, the authorities had difficulty in obtaining convictions through the courts as most juries took this view even then. Whilst it is probably true that most smuggling endeavours were carried out with no physical harm to anybody this was not always the case. Every instance reduced government income - customs and excise duties being the principal form of raising funds - at a time when the country was almost constantly at war. Additional costs were incurred in trying to control it.

Christchurch had sufficient interest in the benefits of 'free trade' to cause proposals which might harm it to be dropped. Even if it had been practical to improve the harbour for legitimate trade it would have been at the undeclared expense of smuggling. After practical improvements to the taxation system had rendered the practice no longer cost-effective - and it was this rather than draconian penalties or superior prevention methods which brought about its demise - there was a sudden resurgence in interest in harbour developments.

One of the most notorious events in the story of the 'free traders' took place at Christchurch in 1784. In July of that year two luggers landed one of the greatest volumes of contraband ever managed in a single run. They achieved this under the eyes of the revenue service whose patrol cutter was insufficiently armed to intervene. Only after the goods had been safely removed from the beach did more powerful forces arrive in the form of another cutter and a Royal Navy sloop-of-war, H.M.S. *'Orestes'*. In trying to capture the smuggling vessels William Allen, the commander of the boat party, was mortally wounded and died the following day. The ships, minus their gear which the smugglers had managed to remove, were eventually taken. A manhunt was instituted for the officer's killer and, a year later following a trial at which the defence hinged upon the detail of where a murder takes place, George Coombes was hanged for the crime. No-one claimed that he had pulled the trigger. His defence against the charge of being an accessory had been that the wrong court had heard the case. The officer had been struck by the fatal shot whilst between the high and low water lines and had died at sea, his killer had been on dry land when the shot was fired. The High Court of Admiralty heard the case. The defence claimed it should have been heard at the County Assize. Joshua Jeans, the local customs officer was later dismissed from the service for collusion.

The tale of the Battle of Mudeford contains all the elements of romantic fiction coupled with those of grim reality. It possesses bravery and good seamanship but also, and in larger measure, cowardice, treachery, dishonest dealing and simple, unremitting investigative drudgery. Smuggling was a trade, carried out largely as a business venture, in which occasional losses of ships and cargoes were an accountable risk. Participants such as 'Lovey' Warne, who used to transfer rolls of silk by wrapping them around beneath her clothes and would act as a human warning of the authorities' approach by wearing a conspicuous red cloak, became folk-legends in their own lifetime. Dr. Quartley of Christchurch is principally remembered for the occasions he was paid in brandy for medical services to the smugglers. For many years he was the only doctor in the town.

The organisers, the 'venturers' who put up the money, were seldom known and even more rarely brought to justice. The owner of the smuggling vessels involved in the Battle of Mudeford, John Streeter, was actually arrested but escaped from Winchester gaol. He fled to the Channel Islands where he was kept in funds by associates who continued to run his businesses on the mainland. He eventually returned home following the amnesty held out during the Napoleonic Wars. His opponent, William Arnold, Collector of Customs at Cowes, predeceased him, worn out in the service. It was he who had seen that the way to defeat the smugglers was to disrupt the landings, thus increasing their costs to a point where the trade ceased to be viable.

Top : Chart of 1785 drawn by Lt. Murdoch McKenzie - part of a hydrographic survey of the entire coast.
Bottom : Part of the Trinity House Chart of 1797. The legend above the River Avon reads 'To Salisbury'.

Few of the strategies organised against the trade had any profound effect. Smuggling continued, with a hiatus during the war with France, until new tax systems and a reduction in duties made it simply no longer worth the risk.

Whilst smuggling catches the limelight during the Eighteenth century, there was still a good measure of legitimate trade. In the year of the battle, an advertisement appeared offering freight and passenger accommodation aboard the *'Dove'* of Christchurch, sailing frequently, if not regularly, for London. At about the same time, the local brewery owned a sloop, the *'Stour'* which they used in trade to Portsmouth. The following year a detailed hydrographic survey of the south coast, including Christchurch, was carried out by Lt. Murdoch Mckenzie R.N. The resulting chart is a valuable indicator of the degree of change since to the harbour and its neighbouring coast.

Around the turn of the Eighteenth and Nineteenth centuries, the Riding Officer of Customs was Abraham Pike. As well as his role as a preventative officer, he was required to note and charge legal cargoes. His journal for the years 1803-4 survives and provides a clear picture of trade in Christchurch in the years just prior to Trafalgar. At this time there were two quays, one at Mudeford by the Run, the other near Place Mill - the Town Quay. During those two years there were one hundred and twenty-eight cargo movements, of which sixty-two were inbound and sixty-six outbound. The same vessel arriving and departing accounted for two movements only if it discharged and shipped cargo. The discrepancy is due to some ships arriving to only discharge or only load part cargoes, therefore counting in only one direction. How many individual ships were involved is not known but it is estimated that only in eight cases are two movements caused by the arrival and subsequent departure of the same ship.

The strength of the Portsmouth connection is demonstrated by the fact that over a third (22) of inbound cargoes were from that port whilst nearly two-thirds (40) of departures were bound there. The range of other ports served and the cargoes they generated or received is very varied. The principal inbound cargoes included wheat, coal and stone. Most cargoes came, apart from Portsmouth, from Chichester and Lymington. A large volume of wheat came regularly from Cowes in specially designed ketches. The milling capacity of Christchurch made this viable. Wheat flour was one of the main exports as were beer (for the fleet based on Portsmouth and, to a lesser extent, Plymouth), barley meal and rushes. This last was important when many roofs were still thatched and the material was also used as a floor covering and a means of making rush-lights. The reed-beds served a valuable commercial purpose. Bricks were also exported, to Newhaven.

As well as 'bulk' freight, there were a large number of part cargoes including furniture, glassware and household crockery. That the vast majority of ships either unloaded or loaded, but not both, indicates that this was one call on an itinerary of which Christchurch was rarely the terminus. The average seems to have been one vessel, either in or out, about every six days. Some local freight went as far as Truro and London. Christchurch at this time seems typical of many small harbours serving a local purpose. It had both its own ships and semi-specialised trades as well as receiving the necessities of life provided by vessels for which it was just one more stop on the route.

This kind of trade was to continue for a further sixty or so years before the railway caused the beginning of decline. From this general mercantile activity, Christchurch was to develop its own specialised trade - one for which the region is still paying. The improvement theme was to return almost continually and a new form of propulsion was to effect Christchurch both at sea and, more profoundly, on land. The rapid developments following the end of the Napoleonic Wars were to have their echoes here.

Chapter 4,
Trade, Industry and Further Plans.

By the end of the Napoleonic wars in 1815, the country was in the grip of the most far-reaching and profound series of changes it had ever undergone. The industrial revolution was, in its sixth decade, altering attitudes as much as it altered travel, trade, transportation and, eventually, quality of life. With the advent of the Nineteenth century an era of far greater information opens. Not only are there more documents, both personal and legal, available, there are now newspapers and, in an increasing number of situations, family tales and reminiscences. The accelerating speed of change means that only a couple of generations back the world was a barely recognisable place. For example, when I was young, an older colleague of my grandfather (who had served at the Battle of Jutland) had met, in his youth, a very old man who had been a 'powder monkey' in H.M.S. *'Africa'* at Trafalgar. It is unlikely that, however recent the event, it will ever certainly be known in its entirety.

Christchurch, at the beginning of the Nineteenth century, was not such a different place from half a century before. There were already, though, the seeds of change planted both here and elsewhere which would soon begin to flower. Even whilst smuggling was at its height, Mudeford was already gaining a reputation as a watering place for relaxation. It marks the commencement of the trend which has culminated in Christchurch seeing itself as a resort as much as a working community. Whereas before, the town was largely self-sufficient, visited only by those with a need to do so - and vice-versa - it was now becoming more closely enmeshed with the country as a whole. This trend was not, of course, unique to Christchurch as it was happening everywhere.

The late Eighteenth century encapsulated the beginnings of the 'romantic' movement in the arts, of which literature was the first in which it was reflected. It was to change forever the way in which people saw their world. Wide vistas, mountains and the wildness of the sea became subjects of awe and fascination instead of inconvenience or indifference. This change in perception induced a changed attitude to lifestyle, a trend towards enjoying a greater breadth of what the world had to offer rather than remaining restricted by precedent. Like so many other, later trends, this was, at first, the prerogative of those whose personal circumstances allowed them some measure of freedom in their choice of occupation and accommodation.

Around the time of the Battle of Mudeford, work commenced nearby on the building which was to become 'Sandhills'. Built to the order of Sir George Henry Rose, the 'marine cottage' provided hospitality to the King, George III, who visited his friend, the owner, in 1789 and again in 1801. Accompanied by Queen Charlotte and their family, the Royal Yacht (*'Charlotte'*, named for the Queen) anchored off the Run during the visit, an interlude on the voyage to Weymouth. The Royal Family had to board the tender via a line of bathing machines on their return as the tide was too far down for the barge to get close to the beach.

In 1807, Sir Walter Scott visited Sir George's brother, William, at 'Gundimore', his house, also at Mudeford. In 1816, Samuel Taylor Coleridge visited William. In 1821 the new King, George IV, called on Sir George. All this had its effect on the earliest phase of tourism in the area. Although sea-bathing was becoming popular amongst wealthier members of society, it did not gain mass popularity until nearer the middle of the century, by which time Christchurch, and its neighbourhood, was already a centre for visiting.

All this was going on against a background of regular trade and activity. Although the export trade in beer reduced drastically at the end of the war, wheat, flour and coal remained along with part-cargoes of household and domestic items. A growing population and the availability of more consumer goods, with roads little improved and railways still in the future, implies an increase in the number of cargoes.

The need for regulation continued, as did the need to maintain the coast-watch. With the end of the war, smuggling began to increase again, though to nowhere near its former level. The troops at Christchurch Barracks, which had been established in 1792, had originally been stationed there as defence against possible invasion. They now served to assist the preventive service. In 1823, Sir George Rose (the son of the builder of 'Sandhills') leased the 'Haven House' to the the Board of Customs and renewed it in 1844. The range of coastguard cottages was built at this time to enhance the facilities, which already included an extension to the 'Haven House'. It was less than forty years since the same building had housed those planning the run which led to the Battle of Mudeford. The public house facilities were replaced by a new building of the same name (since replaced again but retaining the title). The original building reverted to being called the 'Dutch' house, an allusion to its possible construction in connection with Clarendon's improvement scheme of over a century before. The Dutch provided notable engineers in the field of marine and harbour works and may well have been involved.

Plans for improvement.

By the 1830s, with the population now approaching five thousand, there were calls for improvements to the harbour's facilities and capacity. In 1836, 'several gentlemen' commissioned William Armstrong, an engineer from Bristol, to survey the harbour and recommend costed improvements. Almost simultaneously, the Corporation commissioned another survey, to be carried out by John Sylvester, also an engineer but from London.

Using the expertise of Benjamin Tucker, a local shipowner and master involved in the coal trade, amongst others, Armstrong surveyed the harbour in detail. Tucker's hoy, *'Pilot'*, was used to make soundings and to chart the channel. Reporting in July, Armstrong's recommendations were considered at a public meeting on November 9th. Allowing that the overall high-water depth was around ten feet, except in a few clearly revealed places, he recommended that Clarendon's jetty be extended back, right through the sandbank, and then continued as a training wall all along the north side of the main

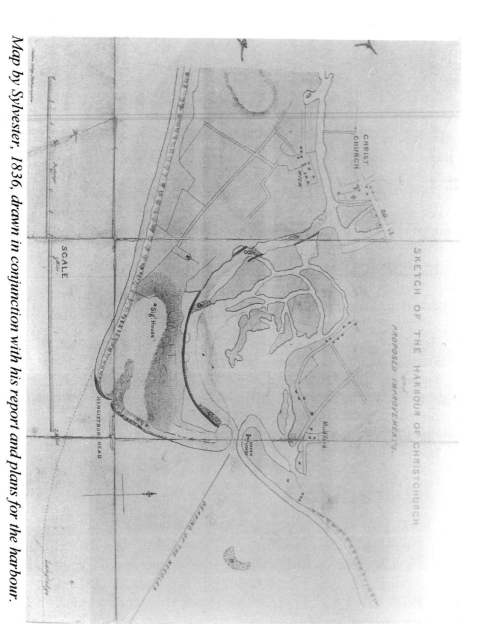

Map by Sylvester, 1836, drawn in conjunction with his report and plans for the harbour.

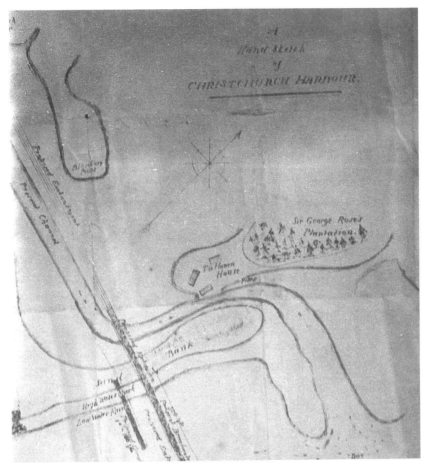

Hand sketch by Armstrong, 1836, showing his proposals for the refurbishment of Clarendon's Jetty.

channel, which would be straightened. A new jetty would be built, parallel to and to the south of that already existing, and the natural entrance be sealed. The accelerated flow of the rivers would then scour the channel and deposit their suspensions beyond the bar. The reflection of Smeaton's suggestions is further apparent in the choice of materials and estimated cost (at £6,000 an increase of 20%). The difference lies principally in that Armstrong did not see any problems in realising the scheme or in its achieving its objectives.

Sylvester conducted his survey in August and reported to the Corporation in September. His recommendations were far more realistic than Armstrong's. He noted Smeaton's ideas and the existence of the jetty but possessed severe doubts that any major scheme would ever be practical, let alone cost-effective. He made the point that it was the depth at the bar which governed the draft of ships able to enter the harbour and to increase that would require piers of such inordinate length and bulk as to render them prohibitively expensive. Provided that the least depth in the channel up to the quay equalled that over the bar, he argued, the harbour would be as useful as it was ever likely to become for commercial purposes. Dredging and embanking, at an estimated cost of £1,700, were his answers to the problem, realistic but lacking the sparkle and excitement that the town desired. In the event, neither plan was implemented.

Interest in improvements was not easily quashed in an age when engineering was producing imaginative solutions to old problems and, in some cases, inventing new ones to solve. The following year, a variation on Armstrong's theme suggested the construction of an embanked harbour for pleasure craft - a marina in 1837! By implication, there were now sufficient non-commercial vessels to make this idea seem viable.

In 1845, there came the first echo of a real new age. In that year construction of the railway between Southampton and Dorchester was commenced. Although it was seen as one stage of a trunk route between London and Exeter, in competition with the Great Western, and was to run via Wimborne and Ringwood, all sorts of possibilities were envisaged as it progressed. Amongst these was a suggestion that a branch be constructed to link Ringwood with Mudeford and there to construct a dock for boats to the continent. Nothing came of these ideas, either, though they were to be by no means the last. Christchurch Harbour was surveyed by Capt. Sheringham R.N. during 1846, on behalf of Sir Francis Beaufort, Controller of the Hydrographic Office. Like Lt. Mackenzie's survey of sixty years earlier, this was for the provision of accurate charts of an area which was rapidly becoming the fringe of one of the world's busiest seaways.

The commercial harbour of Christchurch.

The regular trade, whose desired expansion had generated the mania for improvement, continued to flourish. The main imports during the first half of the century seem to have been coal and limestone. This material was burnt in kilns and dowsed for conversion to slaked lime which was then used as a soil dressing. The kilns in Christchurch Harbour were situated alongside the channel running along the northern shore of Hengistbury Head.

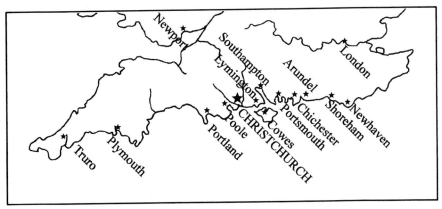

Southern British ports which Christchurch traded with during the years 1803-4.

In addition to the lime-kilns, the Haven and Town quays, there were a number of other landing places. Coal was regularly unloaded at Fisherman's Bank on the northern side of the harbour whilst there was another wharf on the eastern arm of the Avon by the Purewell (and Southampton) road. The old quay near the works was gradually being superseded by use of the mud-berth at Quomps on the Stour. This land had been given for a quay a century and a half earlier and was upgraded about this time by the construction of a timber-revetted quay wall. Christchurch Brewery, up for sale in 1839, included in its particulars the convenience of the Quay '... whence shipment may be made to all parts of the United Kingdom...'. Later in the century a coal store was constructed there to hold stocks for the nearby steam pumping station.

Bailey's Directory for the town in 1784 shows the existence of a Mr. Holloway, boatbuilder. At the time of the wars with France, and possibly earlier, boats were being constructed at the Black House on the sandspit at Hengistbury. The best known of these were the 'guinea cutters', fast, many-oared rowing boats which could outrun the revenue service cruisers and were ideal for transporting contraband, including bullion, during the war. G. Holloway appears in Pigot's Directory, for 1830, as a plumber and glazier. By 1851 George Holloway is being described as a boatbuilder. Whilst this may be seen as following in his father's footsteps, it seriously understates the work Holloway was undertaking.

In both 1842 and 1847, Holloway had laid down merchant ships at a yard beside the Black House. The former was 'Viscountess Canning' which appears in the supplement to Lloyd's Register of Shipping for that year under the ownership of Forster & Co. of London, having already been sold. It was common at the time to construct ships as speculative ventures and search for a buyer whilst building. 'Viscountess Canning' was a brig of 193 tons with a yellow-metal sheathed hull for protection against ship-worm in tropical waters. She traded to African ports for the first eight years of her life. Seriously damaged in either '47 or '48, she was repaired and then traded in the Channel, North Sea and Baltic. In 1858, at the end of the ten-year registration as category A1, renewed after her repairs, she returned to the Channel trade where she remained, based in Guernsey, until being wrecked on a voyage to Yarmouth in 1861.

The second of Holloway's ships was *'Enterprize'*, built for him by Ellwood Day at a cost of twenty-six shillings per ton. She was launched in August 1848, having been sold on the stocks to S. Tice of Southampton. Another brig, she was 94 feet between perpendiculars, 21 feet 8 inches in the beam and had a depth in hold of 15 feet. Her burden was measured at 253 tons and she was also yellow-metalled. In the year of her launching she was registered in London and traded between Shields and the Mediterranean which continued until 1856 when she was re-metalled and felted. Sold the following year, she retained her London registration serving in the coastal trade to Bristol. In 1864, she was condemned.

Both ships were much too large to serve their port of construction and neither ever visited it. Their careers are typical of hundreds of middle-size merchant ships of the period but they remain the largest vessels built at Christchurch.

During the earlier years of the Nineteenth century, the coal trade was largely in the hands of the Bemister and Tucker families. In 1842, Benjamin Tucker's boat *'Pilot'* was wrecked and his place in the trade appears to have been taken by another Holloway, John Edward. J. E. Holloway had come from Ryde on the Isle of Wight where he had been an architect. At the age of twenty-one, he was operating as a general trader, principally shipping limestone. For this he used a fleet of barges which were easily adapted to carrying coal. This was brought to Christchurch from Southampton where it had arrived by collier from South Wales and the Tyne. To ballast his vessels on the return trip, Holloway used ironstone boulders gathered from the foreshore of Hengistbury Head. Finding that he could sell-on this material to the colliers - instead of simply casting it overboard, as was usual with unwanted ballast - he quickly grasped the commercial implications of the situation. Thus began an industry which, over the subsequent twenty-three years, did such damage to the natural defences of the Head and harbour that the price is still being paid.

The Hengistbury Head Mining Company.

Prior to the 1840s, Hengistbury Head was protected from assault by the sea by a mass of ironstone 'doggers', or boulders, at its base and a reef of ironstone stretching out to sea in a south-easterly direction. The Head, itself, contained a number of further layers of ironstone. Since the beginning of accurate mapping, the basic form of the headland and harbour entrance had remained largely unchanged. This was about to alter.

Aerial view of Hengistbury Head

In 1847, Holloway applied to Sir George Gervis for a lease to remove the doggers. Gervis was claiming foreshore rights for himself from this time, on the basis of being Lord of the Manor, although not necessarily the owner. The lease was granted the following year and accessible stone began to be removed, being transferred from the beach to the loading place, probably near the lime kiln, by cart. In 1849 the Hengistbury Head Mining Company was registered in the names of Samuel Homfray and Mary Ann Davis, said to be resident in South Wales. Within two or three years the company found it economic to build a tramway to assist in transporting the stone to the landing. There are no figures to indicate the amount of stone taken during this early phase but, by around 1852, most of the loose material and that which could be won from the reef at low water had been removed. Mining now commenced into the base of the cliffs.

 *Holloway's letterhead showing his steamer 'Carrs' and barges.*

This activity was already beginning to have an observable effect on both the Head and the Run. Sir George Rose had written to the Admiralty in 1851 regarding the erosion which was already beginning to change the character of the harbour entrance. The southern sand bank was extending northwards, overlapping the northern and diverting the rivers around the eastern side of Mudeford spit. Three years later, a memorial was sent by the corporation of Christchurch expressing concern over the same issue. The matter had been hotly debated and agreed with a majority of one, that of James Druitt, who wrote the document which was despatched on May 17th, 1854. Within two months of receiving this, the Admiralty Secretary established an enquiry into the matter to be investigated by Capt. Vetch R.N. The Admiralty's worry was in the loss of shelter from south-westerly winds for ships in Christchurch Bay. They had received a number of memorials from ships' masters to the effect that the Head was reducing in size and that Old Harry rocks, off Purbeck, were now visible from previously sheltered anchorages. All this had occurred within a matter of six years. In the same year J. E. Holloway became Manager of the company, having previously acted as its agent.

Capt. Vetch reported in September 1854: 'Whatever value the stones may possess', he concluded, 'it will entail costs one hundred times greater to compensate for the evil done.' He recommended that further removal of ironstone should be immediately outlawed. In spite of all this the work continued. On June 17th, 1855, Sir George Rose died, leaving Druitt to lead the fight alone. Although he and Capt. Vetch had become friends and allies, Vetch could only act within the limit of his instructions. During 1856, notices were issued ordering a stop to the removal of stone from below the high water line. Druitt was appointed prosecuting agent on behalf of the Admiralty. This made little difference as most of the worthwhile material from that area had already gone. That year, however, an unsuccessful prosecution was mounted against three men for 'malicious trespass' and taking away ironstone.

In the face of opposition and the law, Holloway now began to quarry into the plateau of the Head itself. A carefully organised system was developed for extraction and transportation of the stone. From the quarry it was lowered down an inclined plane to sea level where it was moved, either by cart or the re-laid tramway, to the vicinity of the kiln where it was loaded. Spoil was hauled away to the west along the edge of Warren Hill and simply tipped over the end. As necessary, the trackway was extended further along the top of the 'batters', which are wholly composed of mining waste. Horses could be watered at the Lily Pond, constructed originally for that purpose. Holloway's coal barges were now bringing in cargo rather as ballast against their outbound journey. He still advertised himself as a coal merchant, his place of business being in Barrack Road. At times over four thousand tons of stone were awaiting shipment. Extraction of around fifty to one hundred tons per day was common. The transport system was becoming overloaded.

By 1855 the company had acquired the use of a steam tug, the 'Carrs', which could tow three barges containing an aggregate load of six-hundred tons. This ship, the first steamer to use Christchurch, was probably owned by Holloway and leased to the company. Later in the decade, the transportation difficulties were eased by the construction of a canal from a point east of the lime kiln across the salt marsh to the base of the Head. An embanked dock was also built. Stone now came down the inclined plane direct to the quayside.

About the same time, blasting began to be used to loosen the stone. This resulted in some horrific accidents, few of which resulted in inquests, let alone prosecution. The workhorse was largely local, crossing from the town on a daily basis. 1856 provided thirteen thousand tons of stone worth £54,600 at contemporary value. This may have been a total figure for extraction to date because, in the following year, the figure was seven thousand tons (value £29,400) and never subsequently exceeded six thousand tons in any one year. Whether these later figures were massaged or not is open to debate, though the value per ton dropped dramatically in the following year from £4 4s. to around 8s. thereafter.

In 1857, Capt. Vetch reported that the work continued and there were rumours that the Head was to be taken over for military purposes. Artillery practice was held on the Head the following year and irregularly for years after. In 1860, the company offered its leases to the Admiralty who asked Capt. Vetch to survey and report once again. Vetch concluded that the company 'demanded too much' for the leases and that they were probably illegal anyway. The Admiralty rejected the offer. Two years after this Holloway and Homfray were accused of failing to fulfil a contract to deliver stone from Instead, on the Isle of Wight, for use in restoration work at the Priory. The result was described as a misunderstanding which took two years and two sessions of Winchester Assize to sort out. Holloway and Homfray had taken Rev. Zachary Nash to court for failing to pay for the material. Nash's defence was that it was inadequate for the purpose by dint of quality and size. The court accepted the latter but not the point of quality nor that the contract had been gained by deception. Holloway and Homfray were described as leading citizens of the town (as was Zachary Nash). Holloway was also a Justice of the Peace and a town councillor.

Less than a year later, Capt. Vetch died but his work was

continued by Christopher Creeke, architect and surveyor for the Bournemouth Commissioners. Between '64 and '69 he monitored and reported on the sea's encroachment onto the Head. In August 1867 a further memorial was sent to the Admiralty regarding their inactivity in the matter; a reply was received in December to the effect that their former responsibility was now within the jurisdiction of the Board of Trade. In September, Holloway had been made Mayor of Christchurch.

1864 is the last year for which figures are available for tonnage extracted. Since 1856, a total of 52,650 tons had been recorded. How much before the record begins, and how much after are matters for conjecture. In 1869 mining was still going on but interest had now shifted to controlling the damage caused by the earlier, beach-collecting activity. Druitt and Creeke had joined forces to press for an artificial breakwater to reduce the effects of the loss of almost one-half of the headland. Both were long-dead when this work was carried out nearly seventy years later. During 1870, the last stone was removed, work stopped and the company finally ceased trading. It has been suggested that the combined opposition of Druitt and his allies brought this about. This may be part of the reason although it had had little effect previously. It seems more likely that the continued low price for the ore, coupled with increasing extraction costs simply made it a business decision.

What did not stop was the erosion of the Head. Although now partly controlled by the Long Groyne at the extreme corner of the remains of the headland, drift and erosion continue down to the present day. The Run, at one time during the 1880s and '90s, extended as far as Highcliffe and often reached Steamer Point, requiring the navigation of a two mile 'lagoon' to enter the harbour. This sand bank was fragile in the face of severe weather and the course of the Run and, consequently, the approach to the harbour, were in a state of constant change. This had a further effect on shore-side property which could find its sea defences lost overnight. As recently as the 1980s, there was concern that the sea might break through the neck of Hengistbury, necessitating immediate and costly remedial work. Capt. Vetch's estimate of one-hundred times the cost now seems sadly insufficient.

The Victorian era and John Edward Holloway departed within a few weeks of each other in 1901. Holloway was buried in Christchurch Cemetery where his monument is surrounded by an iron railing.

The arrival of the railway and international proposals.

It is sometimes implied that major technological advances cause an almost instant cessation of whatever system was in operation before. The railway is a good example of this myth. The first line in the area, between Southampton and Dorchester, opened in 1847. The connection from Ringwood to Christchurch opened fifteen years later, on November 15th, 1862. This line was single track and was intended to be extended into Bournemouth. This did not happen until February, 1870. In some cases, the development of railways was anything but the manic affair it had been earlier in the century. Forty years after the first train arrived at Christchurch, coal was still being regularly shipped into the harbour by barge.

In the long term, the railways had a profound effect, not only on the transportation of freight, but also on the availability of travel to a huge proportion of the population which, in earlier generations, would have been limited to the distance they could walk. The lines approaching from the east were those of the London and South Western Railway. On the north-western side of Bournemouth, the main L & SWR line at Wimborne was connected to the Somerset and Dorset Joint Railway in 1863. This was soon extended into Bournemouth, providing the town with two non-connected stations, both of which could be reached from the direction of Southampton, but still no direct route to London. This was resolved in 1888 when a 'direct' line was opened between Brockenhurst and Christchurch, enabling Waterloo trains to reach Bournemouth without detouring via Ringwood. The Christchurch to Ringwood line now became an insignificant branch and lapsed back into the obscurity which it had

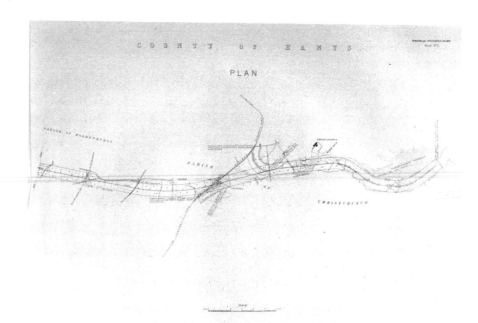

The Wimborne and Christchurch Railway Plan of 1885.

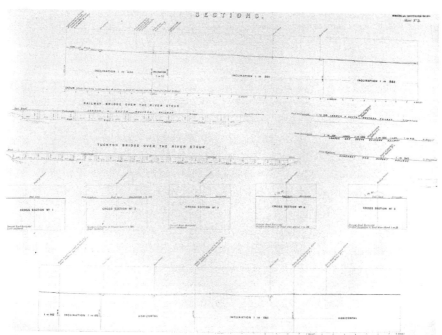

Sections of the proposed railway from the above plan.

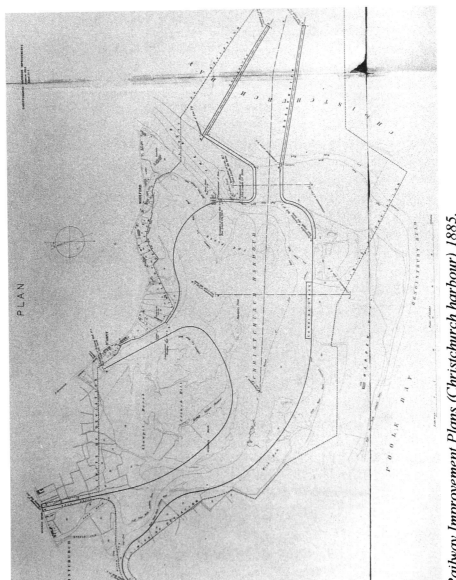

Railway Improvement Plans (Christchurch harbour) 1885.

enjoyed before the original extension to Bournemouth.

Before this happened there was proposed what was to be the last major plan for the improvement of Christchurch Harbour. It came from the Wimborne and Christchurch Railway (a company which seemed to exist principally in the minds of the directors of the Somerset and Dorset) and was intended to finally link the Bristol and English Channels by railway. In reality, all the major railway undertakings operating on, or to, the south coast had maritime divisions or connections except the S & D. This was their proposal to gain equality. The line was to run from Wimborne station across open country until it met the main Ringwood - Christchurch - Bournemouth line near Iford on the lower Stour. It would then ignore Christchurch town, cross the main line and head largely south-eastwards, crossing and re-crossing the Stour, until it reached Tuckton. From there it would continue past Wick village, on the river side, cross Wick Hams and Barn Bight on an embankment, run along the north side of Hengistbury Head and terminate at a station near the site of the lime kiln.

A quay was to be built next to the station, complete with warehouses and other facilities. From here, steamers would operate both along the coast and to Cherbourg, on the Cotentin peninsula. Hengistbury would regain its continental trade after a break of a little under two millennia. To facilitate the required depth of water, the whole harbour would be embanked and a new entrance, protected by thousand foot long jetties, would be constructed. The new harbour would be regularly and comprehensively dredged. Improved quays would be provided at Christchurch town.

The proposal was lodged in the Private Bill Office of Parliament for the 1885 session. When the Standing Orders Examiner came to hear it, in January, the promoters failed to attend, thus signifying that they did not intend to proceed. The harbour has been free from threats of improvement ever since.

Pleasure boats and excursions.

The influences of mass travel, more leisure time and the existence of trading vessels sometimes available for other purposes, made the development of pleasure cruises inevitable. The visits by royalty aboard their yachts earlier in the century are in a different category, as was the arrival of Prince Arthur aboard the paddle-steamer *'Vivid'* in 1862. From 1820 guides to the amenities of the town stressed the availability at Mudeford of pleasure boats capable of secure passages to the Isle of Wight, Southampton and further afield. These were principally for private charter but, from the 1850s, there were organised, public excursions.

One of the early participants in this trade was the *'Diver'*, owned and commanded by George Derham and usually in general trade. From 1858, the ship undertook more or less regular excursions to Swanage and elsewhere as well as to the various fleet reviews in Spithead between '56 and '73. The events surrounding the excursion to the review of 1856, commemorating the conclusion of the Crimean War, indicates the flavour of these events. The visit occasioned a brief but incisive correspondence in the 'Christchurch Times' due to different perceptions of an incident between the *'Diver'* and another, temporary excursion vessel, Hengistbury Mining Company's steamer *'Carrs'*.

Tickets for both had been on sale from agencies for some weeks before the visit. Both vessels were to depart from Haven Quay, *'Diver'* at 5.00 am., *'Carrs'* at 7.00, amended later to 7.30. The fare for travelling aboard *'Diver'* was three shillings whilst no fare was stated for *'Carrs'*, although a landing at Ryde, Isle of Wight, was promised. The advertising for the *'Carrs'* appears to aimed at the 'higher' end of the market, but this may be Victorian hyperbole. *'Diver's'* notifications are simple and to the point. Each collected its favoured clientele and sailed according to its timetable. The day was clear and the breeze light. Off Yarmouth, passengers on *'Carrs'* saw *'Diver'* apparently becalmed. She seemed to be signalling for a tow which *'Carrs'* refused to offer. Having personally reviewed the fleet and returned safely home, one of *'Carrs'* passengers, signing himself 'an eye-witness' penned a vitriolic letter to the 'Christchurch Times' which, had there been any injury, would have added a degree of insult. Describing the sight of *'Diver'* as a '...piteous spectacle...' with '...wings...sadly clipped' he roused the partisan ire of at least one of the sailing vessel's passengers. This correspondent wrote that 'no true account' of the excursion had yet been published, went on to praise the qualities of *'Diver's* master and pointed out that his passengers, at least, had enjoyed the fireworks which concluded the review some time after *'Carrs'* had left for Christchurch. It appears that the enjoyment of the excursion was not solely confined to the duration of the voyage.

The Royal Yacht had carried not only Queen Victoria and members of the Royal Family, but also Sir Edmond Lyons, commander of the Black Sea fleet during the Crimean campaign. Sir Edmond lived at 'Whitehays' in Burton village, just outside Christchurch, and was given a triumphal entry into the town upon his return.

Sailing Races in Christchurch Harbour in the mid 1890s.

Reception of Admiral Lyons in Christchurch, 1856. Lyons had commanded the fleet during the Crimean War. His home was in the nearby village of Burton.

Aerial view of Christchurch Harbour from the east. The Priory, Stanpit Marsh, The Run and Hengistbury Head with Holloway's facilities are all visible.

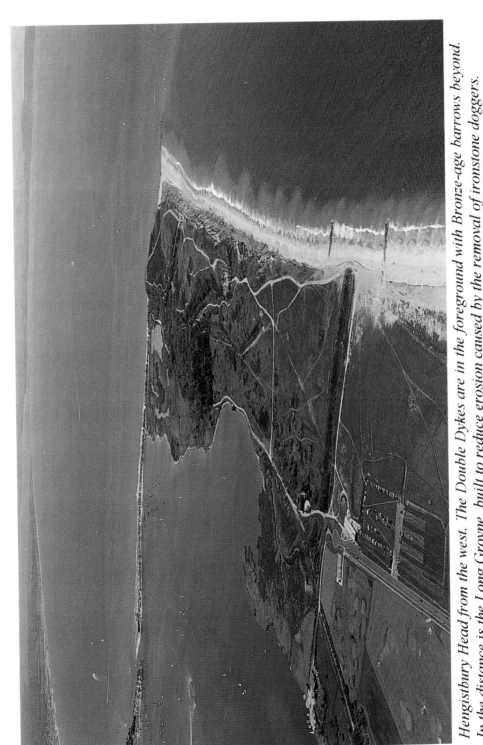

Hengistbury Head from the west. The Double Dykes are in the foreground with Bronze-age barrows beyond. In the distance is the Long Groyne, built to reduce erosion caused by the removal of ironstone doggers.

Iford Bridge in the latter part of the Nineteenth century.

In addition to charter and public excursions, there were increasing numbers of private yachts, both sail and steam, based in the harbour. Where racing was concerned, owners often chose to hire crews but this gradually changed during the later Nineteenth century, particularly for smaller boats. The pleasure of sailing for its own sake was an experience enjoyed by an expanding group of non-professional sailors. By the mid-1870s there were around forty privately-owned yachts at Christchurch and Mudeford of which at least two were steamers. Most of the sailing craft were in the fifteen to twenty-five foot range though a number were larger. This size restriction, in an age of relatively heavy materials and deep drafts, is a reflection of the depth of the harbour. Christchurch Sailing Club was firmly established by the end of the century, as were the annual regattas.

Wrecks, close runs and lifeboats.

An auction was held at Christchurch on February 11th, 1779, to dispose of the remains, gear and cargoes of two Spanish brigs, *'Nostra Senora del Carmen'* and *'San Juan Baptista'* which had been wrecked late the previous year. By no means the first ships to come to grief along this part of the coast, (the supposed Roman wreck may not even possess that honour), their end indicates one of the consequences of a busy shipping lane and recognised landfall combined with peculiar tides, gently shelving bays and steep, underwater ledges.

The Nineteenth century witnessed a number of wrecks and strandings as well as some close calls and acts of outstanding gallantry. In 1809, for instance, a troopship bringing home over one hundred soldiers from the Peninsula War, sank in Christchurch Bay. Her whole complement were saved by fishermen from Mudeford acting in a long and continuing tradition. A specially built life-saving boat was stationed at Mudeford from 1802. This vessel was privately-owned and manned by fishermen.

The Royal National Institution for the Preservation of Life from Shipwreck was formed in 1824 and took over the organisation and extension of existing rescue services. These services were then, and remain, wholly voluntary in both funding and membership aspects. That same year the Institution gave its first Gold Medal for valour to Capt. Freemantle of Christchurch for his efforts in saving the crew of a Swedish brig which sank in the bay.

On November 29th, 1838, the ship *'Herman Julius'* of Uleaborg (Oulu) went ashore at Chewton Bunny with the loss of one of her crew. December 11th of the following year saw the loss of the Aberdeen barque, *'Wemyss'* (Capt. Wier), on Hengistbury Head with the loss of her entire cargo of wheat although her people were saved.

In 1868, the loss of two of the three crew of a local fishing boat caused a new, self-righting life-boat to be stationed at Mudeford. The third crew member had been saved by Lord Bury and Charles Pride launching the first boat to hand, in spite of the conditions, and rowing out to help. The provision of the new, sixteen-foot boat was organised by the Royal Humane Society, who also awarded Silver Medals to Lord Bury and Mr. Pride. The cost was covered by Donald Nicoll, MP for Frome and the boat had been built by Whites of Cowes. It was suggested that it be named for Lord Bury. In 1870, it was launched for the first time in earnest, to render service to a large brig which found itself, as dawn rose, embayed close under Hengistbury Head. A heavy sea was running and the brig, in attempting to stand away from the breakers, missed stays (failed to turn across the wind) and was in danger of going aground. The life-boat stood by her as she then attempted to clear the end of Hengistbury Head which she managed with only a few feet to spare.

Less fortunate was the schooner *'Ocean Maid'* from Caernarfon, with a cargo of slates, which ran aground on Beer Pan rocks in March, 1881. She was aground for twenty-four hours before she could be re-floated on the tide. In 1886, a further medal was given by the Royal Humane Society to Mrs. Emily Stride for rescuing one of the occupants of a boat which capsized in the harbour near Mudeford spit. Today, one could walk to shore from the spot without wetting one's knees. Clearly, the harbour was deeper then. Two years later, the shore was scattered with barrels of petroleum from the barque

'Nor' which had sunk off the Isle of Wight, thirty miles away, after a collision.

The loss of the 'Marie Therese', December 1898. First aground but apparently undamaged; the crew being winched ashore by bosun's chair; finally, 'Marie Therese' the following day.

On November 24th, 1898, the French barque *'Bon Mere'* ran aground on Hengistbury but was towed off, little damaged, by a tug. Thirty-four days later, on December 28th, a sister ship ran onto the Head during a south-westerly gale. She was the steel-built *'Marie Therese'* (Capt. Bevan), which had left Le Havre on Boxing Day bound for Martinique with a cargo of patent fuel briquettes. Beating right across the channel in an attempt to gain distance to the west, her captain had finally decided to turn and run before the gale. She came ashore within half-a-mile of the place that her predecessor had struck. From the same port and company, *'Marie Therese'* was less fortunate in the outcome. Although superficially undamaged, she filled with water and broke her back within a few days and was declared a total loss. All her crew were rescued by rocket apparatus which fired a line from the cliffs to the wreck. Hers was the final stranding of the century.

The twilight of trade.

The arrival of the railway during the 1860s had little immediate effect on the level of maritime trade using the harbour. As the century passed and the population expanded, though, more and more imports came to the town by train and correspondingly less by sea. The development of Bournemouth as a resort further contributed to the decline. Once easy connections were established, passengers could just as easily travel on to Bournemouth as alight at Christchurch. The station became, for many, just another on the journey down from Waterloo. The excursion trade, although essentially local, suffered as boats now began to call at Bournemouth's piers rather than the difficult Haven Quay.

Even so, in 1883 there were still a number of ships in regular trade. In that year the Run was considerably shortened by a storm breaching the sandbank and easing the approach to the harbour mouth. Holloway's efforts, as well as the railway, had their effect on the level of trade. Amongst the ships listed as having called in the few weeks between the breach and the compilation of the list were *'Charlotte'* and *'Olive Branch'*, both regular visitors in the coal and general trades,

78

together with *'Peter'* (in the same fleet as *'Charlotte'*), *'Alpha'*, *'Star'*, *'Pearl'* and *'Tim Whiffler'*.

In 1888, the Municipal Reform Act, which established Bournemouth as a borough and set the boundary down the middle of the harbour, required boroughs to maintain good roads. In April 1898, Christchurch Borough Council invited tenders for a supply of Guernsey granite to be 'delivered by boat to Christchurch Quay'. By July, five replies had been received regarding granite and one for Cherbourg quartzite. Three of this total were for delivery by railway. In the event, the quartzite tender was accepted as, at 9 shillings and 9 pence per ton, it was the cheapest by 2 shillings per ton.

'Charlotte' entering Christchurch Harbour (c 1900).

By this time the quay had been improved over the mud-berth it had been earlier and a coal store had been erected on it, mainly to provide supplies for the nearby pumping station. Trade continued to decline and the last two ships to serve the harbour regularly were *'Peter'* and *'Charlotte'*, both colliers owned by the Bemister family. They also leased the ground for the coal store and, during the 1890s, there was a running dispute between them and the corporation regarding responsibility for repairs and the safety of the building. Throughout the last two decades of the century the Council debated the reasons for the decline in trade and the improvements needed to reverse it. These included deepening the water at the quayside, re-fendering the quay itself and charging the Sailing Club for encroachment into its waters. The Club's offer of 2 shillings and sixpence a year was accepted. None of this increased the number of ships calling. Trade to the Quay continued, though, into the Twentieth century.

Mr. H. Bemister, son of the coal fleet's owner, recalled, many years later, a typical arrival of *'Charlotte'*; 'She would arrive in the bay and stand off. After a few days, Dad would take me in the pony and trap to Mudeford and we'd go out to her. One of the fishermen would row us out in a pot boat. Dad would hammer on the side and, from below, this bearded head would appear.

'When are you taking her in?'

The master would say 'When wind and tide suit', always the same answer.

'But you've been here a week!'

'When wind and tide suit.'

Dad would never go on board. He'd inherited the ship and another one but never went on board.'

When wind and tide did suit, Dick Selwood would sail her a

little way into the harbour. She had a boy on board - the rest of the crew. They had a big dinghy, about fourteen or fifteen feet. The boy would scull the dinghy ahead with the anchor in it and then drop the anchor. Dick would wind on the winch and bring the barge up to her anchor. They'd put it back in the dinghy and scull it out again. The 'Charlotte' was so heavily laden that she didn't drift much with her sails down. There were no engines in those days. That's how they got her up to the quay. She was unloaded with baskets.'

'Charlotte' was a West Country barge built at Topsham on the Exe, in 1871, and registered in Poole. She was sixty-nine feet in length (between perpendiculars), nineteen feet in the beam and had a depth in hold of six feet eight inches. She was measured at sixty tons. She first visited Christchurch the following year and, from then on, brought in a total of thirty-four thousand tons of coal, mainly from Portsmouth. When, on November 23rd, 1906, Capt. Selwood guided her away from the Quay for the last time, two millenia of regular maritime trade came to an end.

Ships in the Run, 1898 - a merchant ketch and a steam yacht.

Chapter 5,
The Last Hundred Years.

Whilst the departure of *'Charlotte'* brought the regular, coastal trade to an end, commercial fishing continued, both off-shore and for salmon in the harbour. Boat-building, also, remained as did the excursion trade, though now within the Run. The harbour retained much of its commercial enterprise, albeit on a reduced scale. As the Twentieth century progressed, so the emphasis gradually altered from these to tourism and leisure based aspects. Two world wars and at least the same number of technological revolutions intervened between the commercial activity of the late Nineteenth and the tourism and leisure of the late Twentieth century. In some measure Christchurch responded to, and was affected by, them all. As a counter to the general trend, there occurred an event in 1938 when it must have seemed that time had slipped backwards. On July 12th, at the height of summer, a trading barge slipped through the Run and proceeded up to the Town Quay. This was *'Gerald'*, a sixty-ton, Thames, 'outside' barge come to collect one-hundred tons of gravel for Newport, Isle of Wight. There have been no others since.

'Charlotte' at Christchurch Quay. The block and tackle for unloading the coal can be seen at the end of the gaff.

The Great War.

By the start of the Great War in 1914, Christchurch was a well established holiday centre as well as an old-established community in its own right. On the main road to Bournemouth stood the barracks, originally provided to house dragoons during the Napoleonic conflict, more recently an artillery base. Since long before the war, artillery practice had been carried out from Hengistbury Head and, during the early years of the century, there had been increasing activity by the Royal Engineers. This included, in 1913, the building of a pontoon bridge across the Run. As the war progressed, a number of Royal Engineer units were stationed in the area preparatory to being sent to the front or during periods of relief. Their time was occupied by training in those areas which did not require demolition.

Several of these squadrons were railway constructors. Light railways were used near the front line for the transportation of bulk ammunition and other material. They had to be capable of rapid construction, re-laying and dismantling. Practise exercises were carried out on Stanpit marsh where the slight remains may still be seen. Holloway's Dock and the adjoining area on the north side of the Head were ideal for bridge and causeway building and evidence of this remains, as well. The War Office was looking for sites with as many features as possible resembling the areas in which these units would actually fight. The tidal marshes either side of the harbour seemed to suit. They only lacked enemy gunfire.

Pleasure boating.

During the Twenties, the number of people visiting Christchurch steadily increased. There were a number of reasons for this. Improving education increased people's awareness of their environment and generated a desire to see for themselves. A generally better standard of living for many provided opportunities which had not existed only a few years before. Transportation was more readily available, both by train and motor-coach, which made day-trips both possible and popular. Bournemouth generated a good deal of this traffic bound for Christchurch, although the town remained a resort in its own right.

To cater for and entertain these visitors, the harbour was put to commercial use once again. Pleasure boat services were commenced by a number of undertakings, operating from landings on both the Stour and Avon, to Mudeford and Hengistbury Head. In 1908, Christchurch Council had rebuilt and re-fendered the Town Quay and demolished the coal store. This now became a centre for the new services. In addition to the various landing stages around the harbour and along the rivers, there were 'tea boats', one of which was based in Holloway's Dock, providing snacks and meals (cream teas at the right time of day, lobster for lunch). A converted steamer provided a similar service near Tuckton.

Many of the early passenger boats, although powered by paraffin engines, were equipped with funnels (which some retained until well into the 1950s) and fitted with 'slipper' sterns. This is a form of stern which appears to slope the wrong way, that is the boat is longer on the waterline than at the gunwale. This extension has the effect of diminishing the disturbance caused by the screw and reducing the wash. The 'slipper' was, in fact, on the waterline, rather than in the water.

Funnel Boat.

In order to operate in shallow water, it is essential to have protected screws which protrude the minimum possible distance below the bottom of the underwater bulk of the boat. During the 1920s, a new approach to this problem was conceived in Christchurch and which is, in developed form, still in use. This was the Hotchkiss Cone propulsion system which had no protruding, mechanical parts. The first vessel to use this system - which drew in water through an intake and forced it through an outlet at the stern, internal, rotating cones providing the motive power - was *'Venture'*, built in the harbour in 1929.

Pontin's pontoon, Wick Ferry, during the 1950s.

Competition between the various operators became rather fraught at times and, around the mid-1920s, a number of them combined to form United Motor Boats. The period had seen fares drop to as low as threepence for the trip from the Quay to Mudeford. A number of the operators were unlicensed and using vessels not approved by the Board of Trade, a requirement if more than twelve passengers were being carried. Gradually the number of operators declined and the service settled down to something akin to the present situation. United currently operate the regular, summer sailings within the harbour between Tuckton and Mudeford sandbank with calls at Wick Ferry and the Town Quay. Services no longer operate from Convent Walk (where the operators once had to reduce all fares by 3d. to compensate for their out-of-the-way departure point) although the Avon is still occasionally visited by 'specials'.

'Venture' and one of the 'slipper' stern boats survived into the 1980s; the former in store, the latter on a nearby recreation-ground. Plans for a proposed local maritime exhibition were delayed and eventually came to nothing. In the meantime, both were destroyed.

Further commercial activity.

The construction of the passenger boats suggests that boat-building continued around the harbour. *'Venture'* was constructed at Bemister's yard on the western side of the Waterloo stream (the eastern branch of the Avon). Shortly after the Great War, Elkins' yard was established on the tip of what had been Convent Meadow, near the sailing club and Quay. Beginning with dinghies and scows, they progressed to general wooden boat building. They constructed many of the passenger boats.

During the late 1930s, a tramway was laid at Hengistbury Head for the first time since Holloway's day. Its purpose was to help repair the damage he had done. After almost ninety years of continual erosion, which had reduced the land area of the head by nearly fifty per cent, steps were at last taken to construct a groyne to reduce longshore drift and build up a protective sand bank. The Long Groyne was completed in 1937 and reached over halfway from Hengistbury to Beer Pan rocks, which had, almost within living memory, once been an integral part of the Head itself.

The Second World War.

By the outbreak of the Second World War, Christchurch had adapted well to the steady social, technical and commercial changes which were being forced upon it. An airfield had existed to the north of the harbour since 1926 and there were substantial boat building facilities, along with the military engineering establishment at the old barracks and the Air Defence Research and Development Establishment at Somerford.

The nature of the harbour and its proximity to the Cotentin peninsula, which rapidly became territory occupied by the enemy, caused some effort to be expended in defending the place from possible invasion. This was by no means the first time that such an event had been considered a possibility. Defences against this eventuality had been constructed in the area since the reign of Henry VIII. Both Hengistbury Head and St. Catherine's Hill had been beacon sites at the time of the Armada. Now, preparations were made against the latest threat.

The beach along the seaward side of the Head was mined and fitted with anti-invasion entanglements along the low water line. Anti-tank barriers were sited at the low, western end by the Double Dykes and pill-boxes were fabricated to command the beach. The high ground mounted a number of anti-aircraft guns and searchlights. Above the beach itself was a coastal defence battery. Although there was no invasion, all this weaponry was used in anger on numerous occasions. Because the pattern of its harbour and rivers was distinctive and easily visible from the air, even at night, enemy bombers used Christchurch as a navigation aid, although actually raiding somewhere else. Hengistbury Head itself was often a target with its searchlights and anti-aircraft guns which were frequently in contention. During both '43 and '44, the coastal defence batteries were in action against E-boats which were being used for minelaying as well as harassing coastal convoys.

The Experimental Bridging Establishment, which occupied the barracks, produced the Bailey bridge, conceived by D. C. Bailey, a civilian designer employed there, in 1941. Following the invasion of occupied Europe, the Bailey bridge made a major contribution to the speed of advance, being used to replace destroyed bridges and being strong enough to withstand virtually any load.

Harbour Defence Motor Launch (H.D.M.L.) built at Elkins' yard during the Second World War.

A major contribution of the harbour to the war effort was the boat-building programme. Many of the passenger boats were commandeered for naval service, often in places many miles away. Not all returned and those which did required much refurbishment. Elkins' yard turned out over two-hundred and twenty naval and military vessels. Six of these were harbour defence motor launches and at seventy-two feet long they were the largest vessels built at the upper end of the harbour. Nearly two hundred of the total were forty foot landing craft whilst the remainder included forty-five foot motor launches and other small service vessels.

The harbour itself was considered suitable only for small craft and none were stationed in it. After hostilities ceased, Christchurch Harbour, like many other places along the coast provided a resting place for several war-surplus launches purchased as houseboats.

Tea / House Boat.

Ferries and bridges.

There are two ferries within the harbour, both long-established and both still functioning. The service between Mudeford quay and Mudeford sandbank, on the Hengistbury side of the Run, was operated with a rowing boat right up until the end of the 1960s. Known as the Fishermen's Ferry, it was available as required until the advent of motor power. Users paid a voluntary contribution, there was no fixed fare. It is said that this was restricted to an upper limit of sixpence to prevent drunkenness on the part of the ferryman, but there is no real evidence for this. As well as transporting visitors to the sandbank, the ferry takes fishermen to and from their craft moored along the main channel near the entrance. The Run is a notoriously difficult stretch of water and it was felt that a rowing boat was more manoeuvrable. The motor launch service began in 1970, after a Christchurch councillor had pointed out that it was the Run being discussed, not the River Styx.

Wick ferry has a history which extends back at least as far as Norman times and possibly to the Saxon foundation of the settlement on its present site. The next lowest crossing point, until the construction of the first Tuckton Bridge in 1883, was the bridge at Iford. During the Middle Ages, Wick ferry was in the gift of the Lord of the Manor and was the only practical means of getting to Hengistbury Head during the industrial period of the mid-Nineteenth century. The ferry was motorised after the Second World War but ceased to operate in 1957 when the holiday camp, whose ground included the northern landing, declined to bear the financial loss it incurred. More recently, it was temporarily discontinued during a dispute over responsibility for the southern landing. It is now operated during the summer months by Bournemouth Boating Services.

Tuckton Bridge was originally built in 1883 but replaced in 1905 with the present concrete structure which was designed to take the weight of tramcars. Before this, the lowest bridge had been where the road west from Christchurch crossed the Stour at Iford village. The earliest bridge here was probably constructed during the early years of the Sixteenth century. Prior to that there had been a ford.

Within Christchurch, there are two bridges across the branches of the Avon and two across the stream which feeds Place Mill. The Avon bridges both date from mediaeval times and the Town Bridge established the clearance, or 'air draft', of vessels proceeding up to Salisbury. Both have experienced much rebuilding and widening but retain their character. It is only possible to enter Christchurch by road, without crossing one or other of the rivers, from Hurn.

Boat-building and fishing, the last harbour industries.

The period following the Second World War saw vast improvements in the quality of life for many people in Britain and a general increase in purchasing power. This was reflected in, amongst other areas, the growth of boat ownership. The factors which eventually led to changed attitudes to overseas travel and the growth of motor transport - both of which were partially instrumental in the decline of long-established, water orientated, leisure pursuits - gave the boat building industry in the harbour a broader market.

Elkins' yard built a large number of yachts, including many Laurent Giles designed 'Vertues'. Later, as the demand for wooden boats declined, they constructed the moulds for glassfibre hulls. The company was wound-up in 1976. The yard, with its distinctive sheds, was taken over by Fletcher Sportboats who constructed a range of fast power cruisers as well as 'Evolution' class yachts. In 1981 Fletcher's concentrated construction elsewhere and the yard was taken over by Tom Lack Catamarans. This company had been operating from Avon Wharf on the Waterloo stream for several years and, in all, built nearly three hundred boats.

Boat building for the private market is an industry particularly prone to the vagaries of external economics. The beginning of the depression at the end of the '80s left only Rossiter's yard, which still builds to order, functioning as the last representative of over two hundred years of documented ship and boat building.

Christchurch was designated a fishing harbour under a schedule of the Fishing Act, 1951 and Mudeford remains essentially a fishing quay in spite of recent and continuing attempts to alter it in the name of amenity. Several large, inshore boats use it for landing and mooring and thus continues one of the last, historical industries of the harbour.

The Mudeford lifeboat.

From 1934 a private, inshore lifeboat was based at Mudeford, built and owned by Mr. K. Derham, the owner of Avon Beach. Twenty-five years later, he was awarded the R.N.L.I's. Silver Medal for the single handed rescue of two people from a capsized fishing boat. This private organisation was subsumed by the R.N.L.I. in 1962, when the shoreboat scheme was instituted. The new, inflatable rescue boat was kept in the open from June, 1963, when it was delivered, until 1964 when the first boathouse was built for it. The present building dates from the late '70s and is the third on the site. The position of the boat-house created difficulties in launching some of the otherwise more suitable, larger, semi-rigid inflatables and the approach to the boathouse has now been deepened.

Like all lifeboats, the Mudeford boat is manned by volunteers and is launched frequently, especially during the summer, to assist mariners in distress. Many of these are private yachtsmen and small-craft sailors but, occasionally, professional seamen also come to grief. In 1980, a Solent passenger steamer grounded on Beer Pan rocks and the Mudeford boat was launched to assist. In their three decades of service, the various boats have been launched 766 times and saved 308 lives. Maintaining old traditions, in 1975 the Royal Humane Society presented a testimonial to Mrs. Sally Parker for the rescue of a man who fell into the Run.

H.M.Coastguard built a lookout on the Head in 1925, close to the site of an old summer-house which, in turn, had served as a smugglers' observatory. This structure was replaced in 1976 by the present building, sited to observe both Christchurch and Poole bays. Warnings and common sense are insufficient to keep many non-professional sailors out of trouble, an increasing number being accidental mariners, blown out to sea aboard inflatable sun-beds.

Sailing and harbour amenities.

The increasing popularity of sailing for both leisure and competitive sport is reflected in the numbers of boats using the harbour and the membership of the various sailing clubs around its shores. At weekends during the summer, the harbour is crowded with craft from organised races to board-sailors and cruisers departing for the continent. Amongst these run the passenger boats and the Fishermen's Ferry. Hire boats, usually restricted to the upper reaches of the harbour and the rivers, sometimes come down almost to the Run.

During the week, numbers of small craft may be seen around the Marine Training Centre, which trains school pupils how to handle boats correctly. Christchurch Rowing Club practises all classes on the harbour. There are several public slipways available which add to the harbour's popularity.

Much of the land on both shores of the harbour is open for public access. Stanpit Marsh, to the north, is popular with bird-watchers and possesses an information point which is up-dated daily. Both quays are open to the public and Hengistbury Head is also a public open space. The archaeological importance of the Head has led to a recent series of excavations which have helped resolve questions on many aspects of both local and international development.

The popularity of the Head is such that there are serious fears that it may suffer irreparable damage from sheer weight of numbers. To reduce the danger, the old freedom to wander at will has been restricted by the laying of new paths and guide posts, together with the provision of information through self-guided walks. Fences have been erected, particularly along the cliff-top, and much of the Double Dykes has been cordoned off.

The damage wrought by the Hengistbury Mining Company is still not only noticeable but continuing. During the 1980s, there was concern that the sea might break through the low-lying neck of land by the Double Dykes and create an island of Hengistbury Head. This has been averted, so far, by the improvement of the sea defences at this point. What further work will be required in the future is a matter for conjecture, except that it will be needed.

During the winter, though, the prospect is very different. Apart from the occasional fishing craft or intrepid dinghy sailor, the harbour reverts to fish and birds. Over these, the ruins of Hengistbury Head look down, as they have done for twelve millennia, on the works of man in river valley and harbour.

Chapter 6,
Postscript - Seeing the Sites.

A surprising quantity of visible features remains from the harbour's maritime past. All repay a visit, not simply for themselves but also for their geographical and historical settings. Christchurch Harbour is well endowed with public open space along its shores and access is free.

With the passage of time the number of surviving features reduces, signs of the ancient past grow fainter, more recent indications disappear beneath car-parks and new buildings. Christchurch is not immune to this trend but possesses an awareness, perhaps more than elsewhere, of the value of its inheritance.

The principal, visible remains are outlined below in a series of five strolls ('walks' is too strong a word). Except on Hengistbury Head, the ground is virtually flat and should present few problems. Disabled visitors may experience difficulty ascending to the plateau of Hengistbury Head and on parts of Stanpit Marsh due to narrow paths and bridges, though neither of these places is completely inaccessible.

Visitors to Hengistbury are advised to take care not to go close to cliff edges, which are often unstable. Whilst on the beach, keep clear of the area directly beneath the cliffs. The rules on the removal of ironstone still apply.

Hengistbury Head - Pre-Roman features.

Arriving at the Mudeford Sandbank jetty from either Christchurch or Mudeford, walk southwards along the beach and road, alongside the saltherns, until the road bears to the west (right). Take the path to the left and climb the steps to the plateau. Follow the main path which runs diagonally across the Head slightly south of west. Although this keeps well away from the cliff edge you can see the clifftop change direction from south to west and at this point there is a

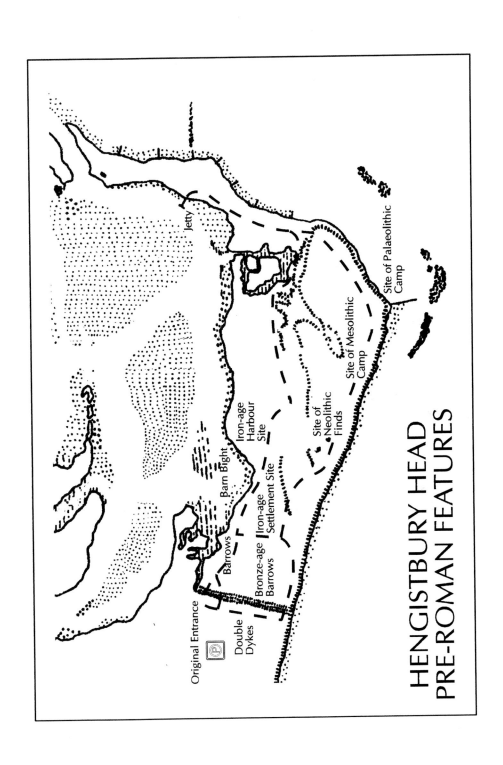

HENGISTBURY HEAD
PRE-ROMAN FEATURES

Jetty

Site of Palaeolithic
Camp

Site of Mesolithic
Camp

Site of
Neolithic
Finds

Iron-age
Harbour
Site

Barn Bight

Iron-age
Settlement Site

Barrows

Bronze-age
Barrows

Double
Dykes

Original Entrance

shallow depression at the edge. This is the vestigial remains of a cove (and before that a corrie) at the top of which the palaeolithic hunters made their camp.

Proceed west along the path towards the coastguard lookout. On your right is a quarry (see Industrial features). On the cliff edge, halfway between the quarry and the lookout is the site of the mesolithic hunters' camp. Both these sites have been excavated and reveal little to the observer beyond the stunning view on a clear day. Remember that their view was very different. Today, you can see the Isle of Wight to your left, separated from the mainland by the broad sweep of Christchurch Bay which terminates at the distinctive Hurst Castle and lighthouse. The nearest points on the island are Alum Bay and the Needles. Beyond these the coast stretches away to St. Catherine's Point. The English Channel is before you and, to the right is the Isle of Purbeck with Swanage and Old Harry rocks visible across Poole Bay. Further to the right is the entrance to Poole Harbour with Corfe Gap beyond. The coast then sweeps back to the Head past Bournemouth and Boscombe piers.

Continuing past the lookout, the path cuts through one of the main neolithic sites and reaches the trig. point, the summit of the Head. There is a bench here (there are many others along the route) from which to look inland. To the west, the head drops steeply away and across the flat land at the base run the Double Dykes, the Iron-age defences. The whole of the harbour is visible with the Priory away to the north-west and St. Catherine's Hill behind. Across the harbour is Stanpit Marsh with Purewell and Stanpit leading back towards the railway. To the right (east) is Mudeford Quay and the Run. The Hampshire coast stretches away towards Hurst, backed by the New Forest.

Descend the steep path at the western end of Warren Hill. In the eroded cliffs to the right of the path, layers of ironstone boulders can be seen interlaced with sand. At the bottom the path arrives at a 'T' junction. Take the left hand direction to pass round the southern end of Double Dykes. Turn right to reach the road which skirts the harbour. Between the path and Double Dykes are a number of gorse-covered mounds. These are barrows, or burial-mounds, dating from the Bronze-age. At the road turn left. Within a few yards you pass two more barrows beside the road, between it and the reed beds. Ahead is the northern end of Double Dykes.

Leave the road by a narrow footpath which diverges gently to the north and, equally gently, begins to rise up towards the top of the inner bank. The path passes through a narrow gap near the top and then onto a causeway across the ditch between the banks. This is the original entrance to the Iron-age walled settlement. It was arranged so that arrivals from outside had to negotiate hornworks and a barbican, under scrutiny from the walls, before gaining entrance.

In front of you is the road to the Marine Training Centre. Walk along its edge to arrive at the road back to the sandbank. Turn left, through Double Dykes, past the barn on your right and back to where the sloping footpath diverged. If you have walked around the southern end of Double Dykes, you will cross this road from the opposite direction. Go on to the original entrance, through it and down the slope, back to the road.

Follow the road towards the sandbank. Keep an ear open for the 'land-train' which operates in the summer. The road re-passes the barrows (now on your left) and shortly afterwards descends to Barn Bight on the harbourside. Along the top of the low cliff are a number of ironstone doggers. This is the site of the Iron-age settlement which, at that time extended well into the area now occupied by the harbour. Continue along the road until it bears sharply to the right and a path diverges almost straight ahead. On your left is a reed-bed. In the Iron-age this was the site of the port facilities. Continue along the road, through natural woodland and beside the saltherns back to the jetty.

This route, suitably adjusted, may also be covered starting from the car-park at Double Dykes. The total distance is about three kilometres (two miles) and the total ascent and descent is approximately one hundred and twenty metres (three hundred and fifty feet).

Hengistbury Head - Industrial features.

Starting from the jetty, turn left and walk along the beach as far as the Black House. Next to it was G. Holloway's ship yard and boats were also built within the ground floor of the house. Walk along the seashore, in front of the beach huts, until you are almost opposite the jetty on the harbour side. At low water you will notice that the breakwater in front of you is far longer and more roughly constructed than its neighbours. This is the remaining core of the mole built to protect the new entrance dug as part of Clarendon's improvement scheme at the end of the Seventeenth century.

Return to the harbour side and follow the beach until it diverges from the road. Continue along the footpath by the water's edge. Cross the foot bridge over the entrance to Holloway's canal. This leads to the stone-loading dock beneath the Head. Originally it was straight but, over a century, tides and weather have altered its course. Ahead of you is a mound by the water side. This is the Knoll, the remains of the lime-kiln. If you scramble to the top, the depressed circular centre, once hollow, can still be seen.

Continue along the water side, which is the edge of the North Channel. The land on your left, west of the Knoll, was earmarked as the railway station site under the plan of 1885. The track would have crossed Barn Bight on an embankment. Where you are walking would have been a dockside. Follow the path around Barn Bight until you reach the road between the sandbank and Double Dykes.

Follow the road west until a broad, gravel path meets it on the left. Follow this path to a further, left-hand junction. This path climbs the Head. Follow it until a path diverges to the left, just before the steepest part of the climb. It has a direction sign for the Lily Pond. Follow this path along the top of the 'batters', mining spoil from the Hengistbury Mining Company's quarry. The Lily Pond, with its

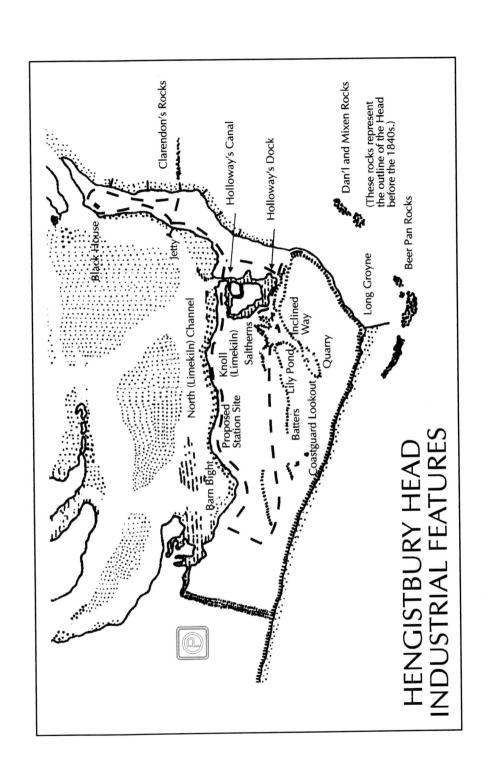

HENGISTBURY HEAD
INDUSTRIAL FEATURES

Clarendon's Rocks

Holloway's Canal

Holloway's Dock

Dan'l and Mixen Rocks

(These rocks represent the outline of the Head before the 1840s.)

Beer Pan Rocks

Black House

Jetty

Long Groyne

North (Limekiln) Channel

Knoll (Limekiln)

Saltherns

Inclined Way

Quarry

Lily Pond

Batters

Coastguard Lookout

Proposed Station Site

Barn Bight

dragonflies and rhododendrons, is where the draught horses were watered between hauling spoil and stone. The higher ground to your right is Warren Hill, the natural headland. Past the Lily Pond, the path joins another at a 'T' junction. In front of you is an expanse of deep water held back by a rough dam at the southern end. This is the quarry from which over 34,000 tons of ironstone was removed in the mid-Nineteenth century. Turn left and walk onto the path across the southern end. Facing the harbour, the ground is split by a ravine probably blasted in Holloway's time and used, after the stone from it had been removed, as an inclined way for lowering stone from the quarry.

Return to the main path and descend alongside the inclined way to the level of the harbour. At the road, turn right. Alongside the road, after about one hundred metres, is Holloway's dock, built to load stone. The dock is the semi-circular gouge beside the road, the remaining mud flats were for extracting salt. The canal cuts across them to the harbour. The timber posts are probably the remains of First World War engineers' bridging exercises. Follow the road until it bears left for the jetty and a path diverges slightly to the right. Follow this on to the concrete sea defences at the eastern foot of the Head. On the beach are hundreds of small, ironstone doggers. It was by removing most of these that Holloway commenced both his business and the destruction of the Headland. By continuing around the foot of the Head you come to the Long Groyne, constructed during the Nineteen-thirties to reduce longshore drift and build up a sand bank as protection from the sea. It points directly at Beer pan rocks, which can sometimes be made out from the broken water over them at low tide. Before the mining started, they were part of the headland.

Return along the shore to the path and the road. In the bushes beside the path and across parts of the saltherns, traces of the tramway used to shift the stone from the beach are still evident.

The total distance is approximately two and a half kilometres (one and a half miles), climbing and descending about one hundred metres (three hundred feet). Suitably adjusted, this route may be commenced at the car-park at Double Dykes.

Christchurch - maritime features.

Park beside Riverside Walk, in the car-park off Wick Lane, Bournemouth. Walk to the bank side path, turn right and proceed towards Wick ferry. On the opposite bank is the holiday camp with the Priory beyond. To reach the southern landing of the ferry, it is necessary to regain the road and pass the head of the inlet. The northern landing also serves the harbour passenger boats. The ferry runs during daylight hours in the summer.

Retrace your steps, pass the car-park and continue towards Tuckton Tea Gardens. A little way upstream is Tuckton Bridge, built in 1904 to carry the tram route into Christchurch. When the ferry is not running it is the nearest means of crossing the river.

Ahead of you is the terminus for the harbour passenger boats, boat hire office and moorings behind a narrow island. From here you may return to your car, walk across the bridge or take the ferry to Christchurch.

Walkers using the bridge turn right beyond it into Willow Way and proceed, via Sopers Lane and St. Margarets Avenue, to the holiday camp entrance. Ferry passengers will arrive very close to this point. Drivers may park in the Sopers Lane car-park or Wick Lane (Christchurch) car-park. From the holiday camp entrance, cross the open space, Quomps, towards the Quay. There is a footpath beside the river. Across Quomps is the pumping house, the reason for most of the coal cargoes to the Quay. Continuing along the riverside and passing the bandstand on your left, arrive at Christchurch Quay. The coal store occupied most of the area of the car-park. The stone quay was constructed soon after the departure of the last, regular trading craft. It now serves the passenger boats and, occasionally, other craft.

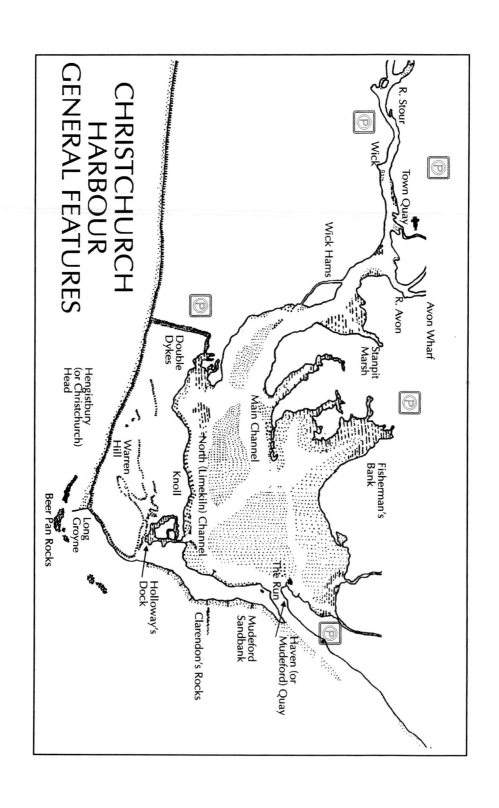

CHRISTCHURCH
HARBOUR
GENERAL FEATURES

R. Stour

Wick

Town Quay

Avon Wharf

Wick Hams

R. Avon

Stanpit
Marsh

Double
Dykes

Hengistbury
(or Christchurch)
Head

Warren
Hill

Knoll

Main Channel

North (Limekiln) Channel

Fisherman's
Bank

Beer Pan Rocks

Long
Groyne

Holloway's
Dock

Clarendon's Rocks

The Run

Mudeford
Sandbank

Haven (or
Mudeford) Quay

Opposite is the clubhouse of Christchurch Sailing Club. Hengistbury Head and, in clear weather, the Isle of Wight may be seen across the river, reed beds and moorings. Facing the Sailing Club, to your left is Place Mill, originally built in Saxon times and powered by a stream which is fed by the Avon. Behind it, across the road, is the wall of the Priory precinct. It now surrounds a car-park and the Tricycle Museum.

Walk along the road between Place Mill and the wall. The road turns right across the mill stream. Opposite is the entrance to the Priory garden. Crossing the bridge you come to the entrance to the sailing club. Next to it is a housing development with its own marina. This occupies the site of Elkins' (later Fletcher's and then Lack's) yard. Turn left beside the mill stream. You are now in Convent Walk, laid out before the First World War to commemorate the coronation of George V. As Convent Walk bears to the left, it reveals more of the east end of the Priory and the remains of some of the conventual buildings. Once beyond the Priory, the Walk crosses the mill stream leat, an overflow into the Avon which is now on your right. This is the site of the 'Works', where the stone and other material for the Priory, castle and Constable's House was landed. The castle can be seen on its artificial 'motte' across the bowling green. The Constable's House, with its garderobe over the mill stream and early example of a chimney, is just across the stream as you approach the mediaeval Town Bridge.

Cross the road and then the bridge (there is no footway on the south-east side). Follow Bridge Street past No. 10, which housed the office of the Riding Officer for the Board of Customs during the Eighteenth and early Nineteenth centuries. A little further along, on the opposite side, is the entrance to what was Bemister's yard. Cross Waterloo Bridge and the road (at the crossing) and return to the slip by the bridge. A little way downstream was Avon wharf.

Return past the Constable's House and bowling green, the entrance to the castle ruins is next to it, and continue until you reach the High Street. Turn right beyond The George, walk down the High

103

Street until you reach Saxon Square shopping precinct. This was built on the site of a Saxon burial ground - after it had been excavated. The Eighteenth century Town Hall, now the Mayor's Parlour, was originally built at the other end of the High Street.

Almost opposite is the Druitt Library. This was the home of the principal opponent of Holloway's exploitation of Hengistbury. A path beside it leads to Druitt Gardens, which is a public space. Follow the path alongside the hall and you will come to a low bank through which the path drops to a lower level. This is probably the remnant of the town's defences from Alfred the Great's time. From here you can bear right, leave the gardens and walk up Sopers Lane back to the car-park or continue back to Tuckton Bridge. To get to Wick Ferry, turn left, go through the gardens and Wick Lane car-park, turn right onto Wick Lane and the northern landing is just beyond the cross roads.

This route may be adapted to commence at any of the locations on it. It is approximately two miles (three kilometres) in length and has no changes of elevation.

Stanpit Marsh - salt marsh and military engineering.

Parking is available off Stanpit, alongside the playing field and the Sea Scouts' headquarters, T.S.'Orestes', named after the naval sloop involved in the Battle of Mudeford. The playing field is reclaimed land; before the Nineteen-sixties, this was an extension of the marsh. Immediately before the parking area is reached, the road passes the 'Ship in Distress'. This used to back on to the northern end of Mother Siller's Channel through the marsh. Next to it is the site of a tobacco manufactory, once owned by John Streeter, a notorious smuggler as well as respected local businessman.

Walk around the eastern end of the building, past the boat compound, around the five-barred gate and into the lane beside the playing field. Pass through the second gate. The marsh now opens up to your left. The gravel path is slightly above the surrounding land but, at high water, it becomes a causeway. After about three hundred metres there is a hut on the right which houses a small exhibition concerning the marsh and the harbour. Information and guides on the flora and fauna of the area are also available.

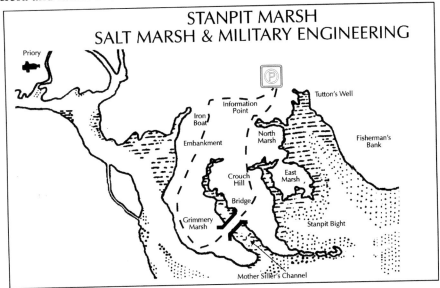

Stand by the information point and look across the marsh. Beyond the channel, the houses on Fisherman's Bank can be seen together with numerous moorings. Coal cargoes were frequently delivered here until the Nineteenth century. Continue along the path between East and Central Marshes. Ahead is Crouch Hill, all of five metres high, which indicates how low-lying its surroundings are. A barrow on the top revealed material from the Bronze-age. There is a bench at the foot of the hill.

The path now crosses Mother Siller's Channel by means of a Bailey bridge. From here the harbour is dominated by Hengistbury Head on the opposite shore. This area is known as Grimmery Marsh. The path now bears right and runs beside a shingle and mud beach. The main channel is close in at this point and, in summer, boats are continually passing, especially near high water. Brander's Bank occupies the centre of the harbour here and across it can be seen the Marine Training Centre and long stretches of reed beds.

Coming off Grimmery Bank, the path bears slightly east of north and runs nearly straight back to the playing field. The various inlets of the marsh are crossed by sleeper bridges. The whole path is on a low embankment which may be the remnant of light railway construction exercises from the Great War. Just before leaving the marsh, the path passes a steel lifeboat surrounded by a fence. Known as the Iron Boat, its origins are uncertain. It appeared sometime between the end of the Second World War and the mid-Sixties. It was probably washed here by storm and high tide. No-one has claimed ownership. Almost immediately beyond the boat is a well-preserved section of embankment, with short sleepers still in place, almost hidden by the turf.

The path now passes through the top end of North Scrubs and re-enters the playing field. Before returning to the car, leave the car-park and walk east along Stanpit for about two hundred yards. Between the buildings is an area of grassland leading to the reeds. On this land is a plaque and the head of Tutton's Well. The Romans believed its waters to have healing properties.

The distance involved is about two and a half kilometres (one and a half miles) on level ground.

Mudeford - fishing and smugglers.

A large car-park occupies much of the spit which connects Mudeford Quay to the harbour side. The promenade beside the Run links it to Avon Beach. On the landward side is 'Sandhills', where George III came to visit. Along here, when it was a shelving beach, the Great Run of 1784 took place. (For all the details of this event, read '1784, The Battle of Mudeford', which you can buy here.) Walk along the promenade onto Mudeford Quay. The 'Haven House' and gift shop are recent. Near them is a stall from which fish may be purchased, virtually straight off the boat. The quayside is stacked with lobster pots and other commercial fishing gear and boats are tied up alongside.

Mudeford from Hengistbury Sandbank.

The Run is deep here and flows, at spring tides, at speeds of up to nine knots (11 miles or 16 kilometres per hour). The light-coloured building with steps to its door is the 'Dutch' House, formerly the 'Haven House' inn, where the Great Run was organised. In the action which followed, this was one of the targets for the Navy's guns. The extension on the back of the building dates from its use as a Preventative Station during the 1820s. The coastguard cottages date from later in the century but were part of the same organisation. The Fishermen's Ferry leaves from this corner of the quay.

Continuing past the cottages, the route passes the life-boat station, open to the public on some days in summer but liable to instant closure if maroons are fired. Beyond this, you re-pass the new 'Haven' and come to the dinghy park and a grassed, open space with benches and picnic tables. The supposed Roman ship was found in the water directly in front of the dinghy park in 1910. From here, Hengistbury is to the left, across the harbour, whilst the Priory is visible beyond Stanpit Marsh.

The distance covered by this walk depends very much on where in the car-park you start. The route is entirely level.

Appendix 1.
Rigs and Types of Sailing Craft.

Sailing vessels were referred to either by type (related to the purpose for which they were intended) or rig (their sail arrangements).

Barge: (Type.) Coastal trading vessel, normally with two masts carrying fore-and-aft sails. After-mast often much smaller than mainmast. To enable barges to work in shallow water, they were almost flat-bottomed and had no external keel. They were fitted with lee-boards, instead, to prevent them from drifting sideways. The simplicity of their rig made it possible for them to be sailed by as few as two people.

Barque: (Rig.) Usually used for deep-sea trading vessels. Barques had three or more masts with square sails on all but the after-mast. This had fore-and-aft sails.

Brig: (Rig.) Two-masted vessel with square sails on both masts. The after-mast also carried a fore-and-aft sail. Brigs were very popular for both the coastal and deep-sea trades. Many were also used in naval service.

Cutter: (Rig.) Originally a large, fast, single-masted vessel with fore-and-aft sails and two headsails. Used by the Customs and Excise services for anti-smuggling patrols.

Hoy: (Type.) Small, single-masted trading vessel, usually cutter-rigged.

Schooner: (Rig.) Trading vessel with at least two masts, all of which carry fore-and-aft sails. Some carried square topsails on the foremast.

Ship: (Rig.) Vessel with three or more masts all of which carry square sails. Fore-and-aft sail carried on after-mast in addition. Sometimes used to refer to any large vessel.

Sloop: (Type and rig.) Originally a small warship, either brig- or ship-rigged, with open gun-deck. Later, single-masted sailing vessel with fore-and-aft sail and one headsail. Most modern yachts and dinghies are sloop-rigged.

Appendix 2.
The Careers of *'Viscountess Canning'* and *'Enterprize'*.

'Viscountess Canning'; Brig, 193 tons, yellow-metalled.

1842	Laid-down and launched by G. Holloway, sold to Forster & Co., London.
1842 -47	Trading between London and African ports under Capt. Courtland and others.
1847	Damaged.
1848	Repaired, re-registered, sold to Carr & Co., Kings Lynn.
1850	Sold to Spurgeon & Co., Kings Lynn.
1852	Reverts to Carr & Co. ownership. Master, T. Carr.
1858	Sold to Mauger, Guernsey. Master, Le Gallez. Channel trade.
1860	Sold to Valpy, Guernsey. Owned by master.
1861	Wrecked on passage to Yarmouth.

'Enterprize'; Brig, 253 tons, 94 ft. x 21 ft. 8 ins. x 15 ft. depth in hold, yellow-metalled.

1847	Laid-down. Built by Ellwood Day for G. Holloway at 26s. per ton.
1848	Sold on stocks to S. Tice, Southampton. Launched in August. Sold to T. Morgan, London. Master, Forbes.
1855	Sold to Griggs & Co., London. Trading between Shields and Mediterranean. Master, Huson.
1856	Re-metalled and felted.
1857	Sold to W. Maddons, London. Bristol and coastal trade. Master, W. Broad..
1864	Condemned.

Appendix 3.
John Taylor's Record of his Wherry Voyage along the River Avon, 1625.

'As I passed up the River, at the least two thousand swans, like so many pilots, swam in the deepest places before me and showed me the way. When I came to the town of Ringwood (fourteen miles short of Salisbury) I there met with His Majesties trumpeters, and there my followers, Mr. Thomas Underhill and Mr. Richard Stocke, Mr. Thomas Ramsay, Mrs. Randall Lloyd, with other, which I name not did walk on the banke, and gave me two excellent flourishes with their trumpets for the which I thank them in print and by word of mouth. At last I came to a Towne, called Forthing Bridge, where (not many days before) a grievous mischance happened. For two men were swimming or washing in the River, a Butcher passing over the Bridge (with a Mastiffe Dogge with him) did cast a stone into the water and say a Ducke, at which the Dogge leaped into the River and sea'zd upon one of the men and killed him, and the Butcher leaping in after, thinking to save the man, was also slaine by his own Dogge; the third man hardly escaping, but was bitten of him.

From thence I passed further to a place called Hale where we were welcomed by the Right Worshipful Sir Thomas Penruddock knight whom we carried there in our Boate and whom, I am assured, will be a forward and a liberal benefactor towards clearing of the River.

So passing in our course by the villages of Burgate, Breamer, Chartford, Downton and Stonely, we came to Langford, where we were well entertained by the Right Honorable the Lord Edward Gorges (Lord Baron of Dundalk, and Captain of His Majesties strong and defensible Castle of Hurst in Hampshire) to whom in love and duty we proffered the gift of our tattered, wind shaken, and weather-beaten Boate, which (after our being in Salisbury, being but two miles from thence) His Lordship accepted, and 'though he knew she was almost unserviceable, yet his noble bounty was such that he rewarded us with the price of a new Boate. I has some conference with His Honour concerning the impediments and cleansing of the River, and I know he is most forwardly and worthily affected towards it, and no doubt, if it be persued, that then he will do that which shall become a Gentleman of his honourable calling and ranke. On the same Friday, we came to Salisbury where we brought our Boate thorow Fisherton Bridge, on the West Side of the City; taking our lodging at the sign of the King's Head there with mine host Richard Eastman, whose brother Thomas was one of the Watermen who came in the Boate thither from London.'

Appendix 4.
Extract Concerning Christchurch from 'England's Improvement by Sea and Land, etc.', by Andrew Yarranton, 1677.

'...let me tell you that I have found out two places, one in Ireland, the other in England...That in England is convenient to build Ships at, and at very easie Rates, and is as good a Harbour to lay them up in as any is in England, and in the very Eye of France. And I desire it may be seriously considered. And that the truth may be demonstrated of what I say, I have affixed...sheets in Maps in this Book, whereby the truth asserted may be made the more clear.

The (second) place convenient for the building of Ships, is at Christ-Church in Hampshire. About eighteen months since I was taken down by the Lord Clarendon to Salisbury to Survey the River of Avon, to find whether that River might be made Navigable: As also whether a safe Harbour could be made at Christ-Church for Ships to come in and out, and lye safe. After I had surveyed the River, I found it might with ease be made Navigable. I then with several others went to Sea several times, to sound and find the depths, and to discover what the Anchorage was. At last I found in the Sea great quantities of Iron Stones lye in a Ridge. For in the Sea, pointing directly upon the Isle of Wight, observing it at low Water, I found that Ridge of Iron Stones was the cause that forc't the ground Tide about the point, which had carried and lodged the Sands so, as it had choked up the Harbour: But the Stones near the Shore lay so great and thick, that they were the occasion of lodging Sands by them, near the Western Shore, and so of preserving a place which is very deep and good Anchorage, and within one hundred Yards of the Shore which gives unto that River the advantage of making there as good an Harbour, as to the depth of Water it will draw, as any is in England, where a Boy and a Cord two Inches Diameter will be sufficient to hold a Ship; the Harbour being a great Inland Lake or Pool, and well defended from all Winds.

When my self and son were well satisfied of the conveniency of the place for a Harbour, I waited upon the Lord Clarendon and some other Gentlemen to Sea, and there did discover to them the Reasons at large, having convinc't them upon the place, of the fitness and conveniency in making a Harbour there. They then proceeded to do something in Treating about the River: At which time I observed two great things that place was capable of.

The First is, At that very place where the Harbour can be made, there may at any time safely come in, and quietly ride at least 50 or 60 fifth or sixth Rate Frigats; and that which is more strange, within three hundred yards of the place there is a hill or Promontory which has an old Camp of the Romans or Saxons, as it is said, which will lodge a hundred thousand men, and in three days may be made so defensible, that no Army (be it never so great) will be able to annoy them, all parts of the said Camp being defended by Sea except about three hundred yards, and that is intrenched by a very vast Ditch, yet very useful; and Relief by Sea may be brought to this place every Tide, and no Party by Land, as it is now, can give any opposition. And to me it is very strange, that notice long since had not been taken of it, and some Forts built there. The Second thing I there took notice of, was, The great Advantage his Majesty might make of that place when the Harbour was opened, for the building of fifth and sixth Rate Frigats. A place none can be better, with these advantages.

First, with the Harbour is a convenient place to build Ships. Secondly, The Timber will be carried down Avon to the place for building, for four shillings Tun or Load; the Timber coming out of New-Forest, the River running by the Forest side, and at present His Majesty sends the Timber out of the Forest to Portsmouth to build, and pays for a Load to Redbridge fourteen shillings, and from Redbridge to Portsmouth by Water eight shillings the Load. Thirdly, This place is and may be made by Art, with the laying out of two thousand pounds upon a Fort, a full defence against any Enemy landing, and secure all his Majesties Ships that shall be laid in there from the attempts of any Enemy whatsoever, and will there be fit and ready almost with any Wind to sail out. It lyes over against the very heart of France, and such Ships may there go to Sea, and be about their work, when others cannot come about, for contrary Winds.

The Third great advantage is, tht there the King may have all his Iron made and Guns cast at very cheap Rates. There is the Iron Stone in the Sea, by the Harbour mouth, and the King hath vast quantities of Wood decayed in New Forest, of which at this time Charcoal is made, and Shipt away to Cornwall and other parts. If two Furnaces be built about Ringwood to cast Guns, and two Forges to make Iron and the Iron Stone be brought from the Harbour mouth out of the Sea up the River to the Furnaces, and the Charcole out of New Forest to the works, there being sufficient of decayed Woods to supply four Iron-works for ever; by these means the King makes the best of everything, and builds with his own Timber being near and convenient; whereas now the charge and carriage makes the Timber of no use to him. And having Iron Stone of his own for gathering up, and Wood of his own for nothing, he will have very cheap Guns and Iron. And all these things set together, this is a business befitting a King to have. And as I said, this Fort will be made, and answer the ends I here lay down, for two thousand pounds, and the Iron works built and Docks to build three Ships at one time for eight thousand pounds. The discovery more particular of the place of the deep Water and Fort to be made, and the Harbour within, with a description of the Camp adjoyning is here in the Map affixed.

...And (I) could say much more of these ...places as to publick benefit, but it may be, and it is not to be questioned, I shall meet with Enemies for saying so much...However if his Majesty please to Command me, I will go to Christ-Church with any knowing person, and there upon the place shew him all that is here affirmed, (and the Reasons:)...

But the King need not fear (objections to a proposed tax on imported iron)...for he may if he please have sufficient of his own at half the rates he pays now for it, and good quantities to sell to others, and made at the place before mentioned near Christ-Church in Hampshire...Therefore if the Iron Design at Christ-Church go on, it may do well; for Store will be no sore.'

Appendix 5.
Smeaton's Survey and Recommendations for Harbour Improvements, 1762.

The Harbour of Christchurch is situated in the bottom of a deep bay, formed between the Isles of Wight and Purbeck, and at the mouth of the two united rivers. Avon and Stour, the passage of which to Sea is between two natural points of land not much above 50 yards asunder at low water, within which points the river forms a large inland bay or bason, which is properly the Harbour or Haven of Christchurch, and is defended from all winds; with these outlines one would be naturally led to expect a good Harbour, capable of receiving a number of large ships, yet, notwithstanding these great advantages, nature has ordered it otherwise.

About a mile or better to the S. W. of the Harbour's mouth begins a high point of Land, called Christchurch Head or Heads, for the Coast, in running further to the S. W. forms another, which makes a double Head, with a small recess or bay between; these Heads, as well as a considerable part of the coast extending westward therefrom, stand bold upon the Sea, the foot thereof being washed by its waves at high water. Those Heads have formerly extended much further into the Sea than at present; but being composed of a loose sand, intermixed with some quantity of loose iron stones, the action of the Sea upon the foot of these cliffs in time of storm brings it down in great quantities, and is driven by the violence of the Seas with the wind from S. to S.W. into the bottom of the bay,and there being subject to no counteraction by the opposite winds, it has not only greatly obstructed the bottom of the bay with sand, but has spread itself to a considerable distance from the shore. It further seems to me that the Harbour's mouth has formerly been much more extensive than at present, having reached even to the Heads; but the sand gradually coming down from the cliffs,and being driven into the haven by the S.W. and S.E. winds, has gradually formed marshes to the N.E. of the high lands, and thereby drove the mouth or channel of the river gradually to the N.E. and again, by the blowing of the sand, left dry at low water, by the S.E. wind, it has formed a range of hummocks or sand hills, extending from the Heads north eastward to the south point that now forms the Harbour's mouth, and has thereby formed a natural bank, part of which separates the bason, now composing the Harbour of Christchurch, from the Sea. The sands thus moving seem to have forced the mouth of the river as much to the N.E. as it can be; and undoubtedly the whole has been long ago shut up, had it not been for the powerful re-action of the waters, continually pressing towards the Sea from the two rivers aforesaid, which, in wet seasons, as they drain a vast track of country, must be very considerable; and indeed, by the power of such a collection of fresh waters, great things may be done, did not nature throw out another rub in the way, and that is the small flow of tides at this place.

The great depth of this bay from the main channel tide, the shoalness of the waters occasioned by the sands before mentioned, and the distraction of the current in going different ways round the Isle of Wight, I look upon to be the most probable cause of the smallness and irregularity of the tides here. It is not reckoned that the spring tides rise more than from 5 to 7 feet, and the neap tides from 4 to 6; so that it sometimes happens that the neap tides are higher than the springs, depending much upon the course of the winds; the tides are said to be highest with a S.E. wind, and least with the wind at N.

I am also informed, that three hours after *(query; three quarters of an hour?)* the regular time of high water, when the main tide in the channel begins to set towards the west, a second tide is formed in this Bay, which is generally highest at neap tides, and that the ebb between the two tides is from 8 or 9 inches to 18; which second tide, proving a check to the reflowing power of the land waters, tends to weaken their force in getting to sea.

From the circumstances before described, viz. the flatness of the bottom, the constant motion and increase of the sands, and smallness of the tides I cannot flatter the inhabitants ever to expect a Harbour at Christchurch of any great depth or capacity; yet, at the same time, it seems to me capable of great improvement, as will appear from a further description.

Between the points I found a considerable depth of water, but as the width of the channel greatly enlarges the points, the depth diminishes, and at the distance of about 200 yards, a hard gravel shoal is formed, and still further out the bar, from the points to the bar the channel lays E. by S. and from the S. point there runs out a sand, which is dry at low water, and extends from the said point on the S. side of the channel, and in a parallel direction thereto, as far as the bar, this view was taken on the second and third days before the change of the moon, so that the spring tides were scarcely set in.

At this time I found 16 feet of water between the points, 4 feet 9 inches upon the gravel shoal, and 5 1/2 water upon the bar; and in the road, which lays about half a mile further out in the same direction, 16 feet water; the bottom is said to be a strong blue clay, the Needles bearing S.E. by S. and Christchurch Heads S.W. and just open one with the other. Within the points the channel turns S.W. by the side of the hummocks before mentioned, and from 16 feet, as it is between the points, comes to 7, 6, and 5 feet.

Christchurch Quay lies about two miles up the river from the Harbour's mouth, between which there are the following Shoals, beginning at the Harbour, viz.

Friscum Shoal, water thereon 4 feet 9 inches, (when 5 1/2 at the bar as above) a loose gravel or shingle 2 feet deep, then turns harder. Granbury Shoal, 5 feet water, bottom soft mud and sand. Saltmard Corner, 5 1/2 water, bottom loose gravel or shingle. The Pick had 6 feet 3 inches water and a loose gravel or shingle bottom. There was no other place in the river but what sounded six feet or upwards at the said tide.

About 1 furlong from the S. point of the Harbour's mouth, towards the S.W. is run out a kind of jetty or pier in a straight line, composed of round lumps of iron stone, which have been brought from the Heads; its direction is S.E. and extends from high-water mark 256 yards; the Needles bear from thence S.E by S. so that it is landlocked thereby a point of the compass; its top gradually declines from the shore towards the Sea, the whole being uncovered at low water, but all or the greatest part covered at high water. Round the end of this pier I found 7 1/2 feet water, and at about double this distance from the shore about 10 feet, (when 5 1/2 upon the bar) the water being rather better to the N.E. than to the S.W. of this line, the whole bottom being sand, and almost regularly inclining from the shore in the proportion above mentioned.

From information I learn, that the aforesaid pier or jetty was erected in the reign of King Charles the second, and intended for securing a better passage to the Harbour, and that for this purpose a cut was made through the hummocks, so as to let the water through the same out of the Harbour, and so to direct its course to the S.W. side of the pier.

This pier, it seems, was intended for the N.E. pier; another pier being designed for the S.W. side of the channel; the other passage in or near the present place was then stopped up with piles,etc. at a considerable expense: this course was maintained for some time, and a deep channel was made by the back waters alongside the pier of 15 or 16 feet deep; but then the matter being deposited, and the force of the land water being spent as soon as it quitted the end of the pier, there still must remain there a bar of the same height as the present bottom; however, as that bottom is at least 2 feet lower than the present bar would make at least 2 feet more water into the Harbour, which must, of course, prove a very great improvement as long as it lasted. But before a long time had passed it happened that the back waters, not finding a passage to Sea sufficiently ready through this new channel, broke over, and forced themselves a fresh passage at the present place, which has ever since continued, and the artificial one was presently shut up by the Sea.

From a due consideration of the facts and circumstances above recited, it appears to me as follows.

First.- That from the tendency of the land waters to open and preserve themselves a passage to Sea at or near their present place, and from the tendency of the sea to shut up any passage made to the S.W. that the present course is best adapted by nature to be maintained; this is further confirmed by the bottom of the road, which laying further out in the same direction, is clear of sand; but as the distances from the point to the bar, and from thence to a sufficient depth of water for an entry to a tolerable Harbour, to which place two piers ought to be carried out to confine the land waters, and protect the channel from the driving in of the sand, in order to render the same effectual; I say, the great length required for such piers appears to be likely to be attended with too great an expense, added to the great trouble and difficulty in moving the gravel shoal before mentioned, otherwise, in my opinion, this construction would be least exceptionable.

Second.- It appears to me that the grand mistake in the former attempt consisted in constructing the wrong pier first; or in other words in making the channel on the wrong side of it; otherwise, for ought that to me appears, it might have maintained itself an open passage to this day; for had the S.W. pier been built first, or what amounts to the same thing, had this been made the S.W. pier, by making the passage on the N.E. side of it, then it would not only defended the passage from the sands brought down from the S.W. by the action of the winds and storms from that quarter, but the sea, by breaking over the top of it, would have tended to deepen the channel on the leeward side; whereas by making the channel on the windward side, it would tend to intercept the sands, and thereby immediately to fill up the channel, had not the superior force of the back water carried it out as fast as brought in; so that I rather marvel that a passage was ever this way obtained, than that it should be filled up in the way it was managed.

That this must be the case in some measure, appears from the manner in which the sand now lays contiguous to the pier; for notwithstanding that it is within 2 or 3 feet of the top, yet it lays on the S.W. side at least a foot higher than on the N.E. Indeed I cannot account for a conduct so absurd, otherwise than by supposing the projector imagined the sands to be immovable, with respect to the Winds and Seas, and not in a travelling state; and observing the strong tendency of the channel to travel to the north-eastward, proposed to stop it by interposing the pier. From this attempt however, though unsuccessful, we may learn how strongly the land waters acted, and what may be done by better management in the same situation.

The direction of the pier S.E. is very good, for vessels may sail in or out with a S.W. wind; it could not be pointed more southerly, so as to give advantage to vessels going in with wind nearer west, than they can now do, without giving advantage to the seas from S.S.E. to roll more directly in, as it would not then landlock, with the Needles, but point to the open sea; its situation is also very good, as it stands almost direct in a right line with a reach of the river, and if a vessel should not make the entrance of the Harbour, they will have the road to the leeward.

I would therefore advise to construct another pier parallel to the present one, but on the S.W. side thereof, and at the distance of about 240 feet from middle to middle; and when this is carried out from 50 to 100 feet further than the present pier, then to attempt to open a passage through the hummocks, so as to turn the water between them, and at the same time divert the water from its present course at low water by a catch dam of rough stones, or by a composition of piles, fascines, stones, etc., by these means a sufficient channel being procured between the two piers at low water, that channel will gradually deepen, and the present channel being deprived of the greatest part of the reflowing power, the sands that are now kept out by the same will begin to close in and in time will form hummocks so as to make an entire stop at high water, and the progress thereof, as occasion may shew necessary, may be helped by art.

By these means the earliest advantage may be taken of the undertaking, and vessels drawing 8 feet water may be brought in at a middling spring tide; and as I would advise the whole to be performed by throwing in of stones upon the same principles as the present pier has been built, the piers may be gradually lengthened, constantly advancing the S.W. pier before the N.E. and it appears, that by extending the piers to double the length of the present, that is, to the length of about 500 feet, there will be 2 1/2 feet more water, that is, there will then at mean spring tide be 10 1/2 feet water, and at neap tides 9 1/2 feet water, which will make a very good harbour for small merchant ships, coasting vessels, armed cutters, etc. And as it appears that an extension of about 250 feet procures 2 1/2 feet water, it follows that every 100 feet extent of the piers will procure an additional foot of water, so that the improvement of this Harbour may be carried out to any extent, by gradually lengthening its piers, as time, circumstances, the utility of the Harbour, and ability to execute, shall suggest.

I do not think it necessary to do any thing to the present pier, till the west pier is carried out as directed, and the water let in between them; but I would advise the west pier never be left till it has got above high water. It must at first be made considerably higher than high water, for as I would not advise attempting to dig away the sand for a foundation, whenever the current is turned against it, it will settle very considerably, and unless a good body of stone is originally laid, may settle so much as to make it difficult to add to the mass at top. It is for this reason I would not advise to make the present pier the west pier, for having had a deep channel on the west side of it, the matter thereof on that side had got sufficiently compacted to a due depth; but was the channel made on the east side, the foundation being there shallow, would be undermined, and occasion it to settle afresh, and require a large addition of materials to make it up to the height.

As the tides are said to rise from 4 to 7 feet upon the bar, 5 1/2 will be the mean, which was what I observed, and as I found no part of the river between the harbour and the town of Christchurch, but what, at that time sounded 6 feet and upwards, except the shoals before specified, all which are composed of soft and loose matter, and of no extent, I look upon it as very practicable, by dredging, to make good a 6 feet channel from the harbour to the town Quay, at a mean tide, which will be very sufficient for all kinds of lighters and small craft. This may possibly be done by the river itself, whenever it gets more sufficient outlet to sea; and much more cannot be expected, without a very considerable expense.

The iron stones now laying upon the sands under Christchurch Heads, are very proper materials for the construction of the works above mentioned; but I fear they will not be found in sufficient quantities, if not, rough unformed stones may be brought from Peverel Point, or Portland,the cap of which is refuse, and will answer as well as finest stone.

As this is a work that much depends on circumstances, it is not easy to make a tolerable estimate; yet, to give all the satisfaction in my power, the best I can judge of it is as follows.

(The estimate is missing from the document but other sources indicate that Smeaton considered the work could be carried out for £5,000.)

Appendix 6.
Report of William Armstrong on Proposed Improvements to the Harbour, 1836 and a note from J.H. Dunkin, Secretary to his Employers.

Agreeably with instructions conveyed to me by Mr. J.H. Dunkin, I have made a survey of Christchurch Harbour, with a view to its improvement by the removal of those obstructions that impede the navigation; in which I have been very much assisted by the attendance and local knowledge of Mr. Benjamin Tucker.

Before entering particularly into the minutiae of the case, I will state, generally, what appear to me to be the principle obstacles to rendering this a commodious Harbour, and which must ever operate, as such, to a certain extent. First. The very flat country, through which the river passes to the sea. Second. The very small rise of tides. And Third. The reflux, or return of the tide before low water, thereby reducing the effect of the stream in scouring the channel. In other respects nature has done much to ensure its safety, being well sheltered by the high head land lying to the South West, and the Isle of Wight to the East, South East, and North East; And if a sufficient depth of water could be obtained it would be a very good and secure harbour.

The only means of insuring a greater depth of water by the operation of the stream must be by confining the river in a straight and narrow channel.

This appears evident by inspection; for all the shoals in the river between the quay and the entrance to the harbour are found in those parts where the river is of the greatest width. With respect to the bar, at the mouth of the Estuary; it is the natural consequence of the confluence of the two bodies of water meeting. The stream of fresh water carries with it a quantity of gravel and other heavy matter, until the current is lost in the tide, where a deposit immediately takes place; and altho' it never can be wholly prevented, yet by confining the stream in a narrow channel farther out at sea, and consequently into deeper water, the inconvenience will in some measure be obviated. From the report of the celebrated John Smeaton, made from actual survey upwards of seventy years ago, it appears that the course of the river has not changed as much as at first I was led to suspect; but on comparing the distances stated in the report referred to, with what I found on inspection, some descrepancies appeared, not altogether reconcileable with the facts; but taking it for granted that Mr. B. Tucker may be relied on as an authority, (and from the very intelligent manner in which he makes his observations I feel no hesitation in doing so,) it appears that the mouth of the river has shifted several hundred yards north-east-ward in the last sixteen years, and that during the last year or two, the change has been greater than at any former period within his recollection. This is quite consistent with the nature of the case, as it is a well known law that all fluids maintain a straight course, and are only turned by an opposing cause; so long as a straight course is preserved, the velocity will have a tendency to accelerate. It invariably happens when a stream of water runs through an alluvial soil, obstructions on one side impel the current to the opposite direction, hence a waste of land on the side on which the stream impinges. By the laws of gravitation this waste increases, not in a uniform but, in an accelerated ratio. Apply this to the lower reach of the river in Christchurch Harbour, as represented by the hand sketch which accompanies this, and it will be seen that the waste must be greater every year so long as the river continues in its present course, unless a change should take place, of soil sufficiently hard, to withstand the force of the current. Here the natural effects are augmented by artificial means on one side, and the action of the sea on the other. By confining the river in a narrow stream opposite the Haven House, its force is increased, and so long as it is suffered in this course, the waste of land on the plantation of Sir. G.H. Rose, and the variation of the mouth of the river northward, will continue. Whatever is done by piles, or otherwise, to prevent the waste of land, must contract the breadth of the stream, and thereby accelerate its velocity in that part, and consequently operate with greater effect on the land below; thus a constant waste is going on, which is materially assisted by the power of the tide, as will be seen by reference to the indented form of the line on the south side of the river from the turn at the end of the sand, or gravel banks, nearly to the bar at low water, as shown in the sketch. The flood tide sets in from the southward and meets the stream of the river diagonally, by which both currents are turned out of their former direction, producing an eddy in the internal angle of the streams; and the tide being the stronger body, the fresh water is propelled northward, and the gravel and sand brought up by the tide, and the heavy matter carried down by the stream, meeting in the eddy, become deposited. This deposit commences at the confluence of the two currents, and goes on step by step every tide, until it has advanced as far as the northwest corner of the gravel bank, when the force of the tide is changed and the river maintains its course. This process will go on so long as the ground on the north side is unprotected by artificial means. I am therefore led to the conclusion, that the original course of the river was on the south side of the pier or breakwater, which is thrown out in the bay, and which had been placed there for the express purpose of preventing the river from scouring and washing away the north bank; and if this pier had been continued a few yards further in land, I have no doubt, it would have kept the river in the same course to this day. If, however, as some would have it, the course of the stream ought to be on the north-east-side, the pier itself would assist the natural effect of the two contending streams, and rather accelerate than retard the evil so justly complained of. I am aware that I am in this opinion at variance with the great authority before quoted, but having the advantage of seeing what a change of seventy years has produced in this harbour, and knowing also that my theory is in perfect accordance with the effect produced in all tide rivers, under similar circumstances, I have no fear of contradiction. This leads me to the point to which I wish to arrive (viz.) to devise some method to obtain a greater depth of water, both in the river and over the bar. In all running streams, subject to deposit of any kind, the only known method of preserving a regular depth of water is, by maintaining a straight course of a uniform breadth, and the difficulties of doing this will always be more or less according to the inclination and nature of the soil through which the stream has to pass. In this case, on entering the harbour, you have first the bar at the mouth of the river, which at high water on the average tide of 5ft. 6in. admits of a depth of 9ft. 3in. next we have Friskey or Mother Sellars' shoal which is 6ft. Grandbarrow 5ft. 8in. Smugglers' Ditch 8ft. 2 1/2 in. Claypool 8ft. 5in. the last is immediately below the confluence of the Rivers Avon and Stour, and partakes something of the nature of the bar, and will always be subject to a deposit, to a certain degree. All these shoals are but of short distance: they consist of mud and fine gravel, and might easily be removed. All the other parts of the river are of such a depth as will afford every prospect of a navigation, of not less than 10ft. at high water. About the centre of the bay, and nearly in a straight line with a long reach of the river, is run out a kind of pier, or breakwater, composed of large stones, such as are lying on the beach off the head, extending from high water about 300 yards as shown in the accompanying sketch. The only account I have obtained respecting this pier is, from the report of the late John Smeaton; but, from every appearance, it has been placed there for the purpose of confining the channel of the river in a straight course to the sea: and I think there can be no doubt of its having been effectual, until a breach was made in the land at the end, in the situation of the present sand bank. To effect this, I recommend that this pier or breakwater be made good through the sand bank; that it be carried up above high water, and continued as far as low water mark on the north-west-side of the river; and that an embankment be thrown up from the end or termination of the pier, 3ft. above high water in a straight line to Salt Marsh Corner, as shown in the sketch. The sand bank to be cut through on the south side of the pier, and by continuing the Pier about 100 yds. farther into the sea, it will produce a greater depth of water on the Bar; and as the course of the river from Salt Marsh Corner to the small bar will be maintained in a straight and narrow course, it will be gradually deepened, so that, in a very short time, this reach which is from its great width comparatively shoal, will be deeper than any other part of the river. With regard to the other shoals, the more effectual method would be by making embankments at low water mark, so as to confine the river in a narrow channel; by this means the shoals would be gradually lessened; but as this may involve too much expense, recourse must be had to a small dredging machine, which is the cheapest mode of excavation, known; the sand and gravel taken out might be deposited on the low ground on each side of the river, which in time would raise it above high water mark, and thus reduce the width of the water way, so that much may be done by such a process towards effecting the object aimed at. By continuing the pier, and making an embankment from the end thereof, to the Salt Marsh Corner, the present mouth of the river would be filled up, by the action of the tide driving in sand and gravel. In order to carry off the water from the Brook Mude, on the north west of the haven house, and of another stream issuing from Sir. G.H. Rose's plantation, I propose to unit them into one channel, to be conducted to a flood hatch placed near the upper end of the breakwater. When the pier is carried out and the navigation opened on the south side thereof, it would be a safe guard, and a great conveniance to vessels entering the port with adverse winds, to have a pier of a similar construction on the southward side of the entrance. This pier would commence at high water mark against the sand bank, and run out in a parallel direction with the present pier, to a distance of 80 or 100 yards: as there never can be any scour against that side, the stones would be mixed with gravel and sand by the action of the two currents coming in contact, in the same manner as the gravel now deposited on the south side of the present entrance, would collect in the same way, and tend to force the river northward, unless the pier should be of sufficient strength to resist it. But of this there does not appear to be any risk, these stones having laid in the same state upwards of 150 years, and, according to the statement made in the report before referred to, have maintained their position against the tide and river so long as the course of the river was in that direction. Should it appear however that the current has any injurious effect on the pier, a remedy is at hand by the addition of stones: the whole of this work may be effected at an easy expense from the proximity of the material, which is to be found in great abundance off the head; an immense quantity may be taken up at low water from the channel extending upwards of a mile from the head, by having strong boats carrying about 30 or 40 tons, with a sort of crane erected on board, furnished with nippers to take hold of the blocks of stone; the vessel would always be afloat while loading and by commencing the work at the upper end within the sand bank, the river would be gradually forced against the sand bank towards the end of the present pier; and when the course of the river becomes too narrow, the sand bank may be cut through, when the stream would in a short time form a channel for itself. I presume the process must be carried out in this way, as no excavation can be made but what would be filled up by the tide; yet much assistance might be given by removing all the sand and gravel above high water mark; so that as the dam is extended the width of the sand bank would be reduced by the waters of the river being urged against it. The embankment should be made previous to the dam of stone, and both should be united, so as to prevent the river or tide finding a passage at any other point higher up, that is between the sand bank and salt marsh corner.

ESTIMATED COST.

Embankment to Salt Marsh Corner
£1100 0 0
24,000 Tons of Stone from inner end of the pier through
      the Sand Bank, at 2s. 6d.
 3000 0 0
8,000 Tons for South Pier, at 2s. 6d.
 1000 0 0
Excavation of Sand Bank
  300 0 0
Drain and Tide Hatch, say
  100 0 0
Dredging Machine and Well Boat will cost about £1200,
      if a Loan of them could be obtained the removal of the
      shoals in the River would cost a trifling sum, say
  200 0 0
Incidental Expenses
  300 0 0

£6000 0 0

Bristol, July 25th, 1836
William Armstrong.

In conformity with the general progress of improvement evinced throughout the Country, and with an anxious desire of adopting some means for increasing the importance, and extending the trade of the Town of Christchurch, several gentlemen held a private meeting for the purpose of taking into consideration the possibility of rendering their Harbour more commodious than at present for the reception of large vessels.

And with the view of ascertaining satisfactorily how far such a scheme was practicable, they resolved to avail themselves of the opinion of an emminent Engineer; and, if satisfied with such opinion, to lay the matter before the inhabitants of Christchurch for their serious consideration.

In consequence of such resolution, the services of Mr. Armstrong, an Engineer of merited reputation and of much experience in the theory of tide rivers, were placed at their disposal. That gentleman has completed an elaborate survey of the Harbour, and furnished the annexed detailed report.

It is well known that the celebrated Smeaton effected a similar survey about seventy years since; and it is a matter of considerable satisfaction, that the views of Mr. Armstrong coincide, on the most essential points, with those of that emminent Engineer; though the length of time that has elapsed since that survey was made, during which a material change has taken place in the course of the river, may account for some difference of opinion on points of less importance.

On a reference to the report it will be seen, that by a comparatively inconsiderably (sic) outlay of expenditure, the Harbour of Christchurch, which from its situation is admirably adapted for security, is capable of being rendered sufficiently commodious for the reception of large Merchant Vessels.

The advantages which would result to the Town of Christchurch and its neighbourhood, from the increase of trade consequent upon opening the Harbour, are too obvious to need any comment; and an early opportunity will be taken of laying the details before the public, by calling a general meeting of the Inhabitants of which due notice will be given.

Christchurch, Sep. 16th, 1836.
J.H.Dunkin, Hon. Sec.

Appendix 7.
John Sylvester's Report on his Survey of the Harbour, 1836.

Report upon the present state of the Harbour of Christchurch, in Hampshire, from observations made on the 15th and 16th of August, 1836, and proposed means of improving the same, accompanied by a Sketch.

Commencing an examination of the channel of the River, at the Town Pier, being at the time of high water, and a neap tide.

At the Town Pier, and in the narrow part of the Rivers, Avon and Stour, soundings gave from 14 to 18 feet of water, gradually shallowing to 7 or 8 feet to the part (9) in the sketch, where a shoal exists, and the bottom, previously compact, is a loose gravel or Shingle, the depth of water over this shoal, was not more than 4 1/2 feet. The channel beyond this averaged 7 or 8 feet for the distance of about one third of a mile, when another shoal (S) is formed crossing the entire Road, the bottom consisting of soft mud and sand, with 4 3/4 feet of water over it. There is afterwards a channel from 7 to 9 feet deep, taking nearly the direction of the darker shade of blue, in the sketch, as far as (M) where there is a shallow of some extent, and a bottom of loose gravel, holding out about 5 1/2 feet of water; from this point the channel deepens; at the Harbour mouth it is from 16 to 18 feet, the bottom being hard gravel, and a bar at about one quarter of a mile out in the Bay appears to be composed of the same kind of material; the depth of water over this bar was found to be barely 9 feet. At about half a mile is the bar (B), an accumulation forming a bottom of gravel next the Harbour mouth, and sand; out upon this bar, being considered at the time in a favourable condition, the water was barely 9 feet; outside the bar the depth of water in the Bay increases, but so gradually that at more than three miles out it is not four fathoms.

From the peculiar situation of the Bay of Christchurch, with respect to the general channel of the Sea and the adjacent land, circumstances arise, hereafter to be described, which seem to entirely shut out the possibility of a Sea entrance to the Harbour from the Bay of Christchurch, possessing the requisite depth of water for general utility.

An early attempt to form an improved entrance to the Harbour, seems to have been made by a Pier at a short distance South of the present Harbour mouth; a work alluded to by John Smeaton in a Report made in the year 1762, in which he proposes an extension of the old Pier, and the addition of another S.W. of it, but it will be evident upon observation, as it was to that truly celebrated man, that very little could be hoped for in the way of a permanent improvement.

As such piers must be raised above water level, at all times, completely enclosing the land stream, and extend into the Bay, to such a distance as to determine the bar, which must ever exist, when the Sea currents and that of the land water meet, at a point where depth of water could be depended upon, sufficient for the purposes of a Harbour of general utility, the work would be of so formidable a nature, that it may be safely stated the idea could not for a moment be entertained.

The present outlet Sea being solely kept open by the powerful stream of the Rivers, the force of the land water becomes the only means in this instance, by which any change can be effected, and if such a stream were discharged where the usual tide of the Channel only operated upon it, there is little doubt but that much might be accomplished, by its force in forming a deep channel to Sea; in this instance however, there is a circumstance which operates very materially in diminishing the force of the land water, and this is the effect of a peculiar current in the Bay arising most probably from the interruption the tide of the Channel receives by the Isle of Wight, by which a reflux of double is produced in the Bay of Christchurch: the direct operation of this, is to pen up the land water of the Rivers, tending to keep it nearly uniform in level within the Harbour, over the intervals of tide, lessening very considerably its velocity and consequently its force out to Sea, from that which would result if it were discharged when the true tide interval only acted against it. This also gives facility to deposit, in that part of the Bay which forms the Harbour road.

The extensive shallow called Long Ledge may be doubtless looked upon as the base of high land similar in structure to that of Hengistbury Head; this being a sandy formation containing loosely imbedded iron stones, and being exposed to the violent action of the Sea, its mass is constantly giving way, vast quantities being driven into the Bay. The accumulation to be observed North of the Heads, by which the mouth of the Harbour has been contracted and driven to its present situation, has its origin from this source, and it may be presumed that as long as any part of the high land remains, there can be little, if any, alteration in the circumstances which keep shallow, and diminish the power of the land water, in forming a deep channel to Sea, in the Bay of Christchurch.

Against natural opposition so strong there is little that art, can do.

The making the River courses straight, or more direct from their confluence to the Harbour mouth, would increase the power of the land water in opening a passage to the Sea, but this effect, determined by the depth of water over the bar formed where its influence ended, would be so small, as to be of little value, without a consideration of the great expence attending such a work. It may be stated as tolerably near the truth, that extending the influence of the land water into the Bay, by enclosing it between piers, and straightening from the Rivers' confluence, a foot of additional depth over the bar would be gained for every 150 feet that such influence extended within the Bay. It is therefore very clear that if improvement in the Harbour is only to be acquired at this rate, it is out of the question, on account of the great expence at which it is to be obtained.

Considering all the circumstances, it is my opinion that all, it is advisable to do, would be, such improvement in the road of the River's Channel, as will insure at all times an equal depth of water, with that over the bar. This work would be accomplished by fencing in the stream, at the points shewn in the Sketch, and as there is no want of a depth equal to the Harbour road, in the river's course, excepting at the shoals before mentioned, which are loose matter and of no great extent, these would easily be removed by dredging, if the improvements in the course of the stream, by the fencing, were not in itself sufficient to do it. The fencing should in my opinion consist of piling, backed by rough stone, the whole expence of this work by which a Channel in the river's course of equal depth with that over the bar, may be obtained and permanently secured, would not as nearly as I have been enabled to form an estimate, cost more than £1,700 and this would be all that in my opinion under the peculiar circumstances, it would be possible to do, if any regard whatever is to be paid to expence, or labour, in the production of a useful result.

John Sylvester.

85, Great Russell Street,
September, 23rd, 1836.

Summary of Shipping for the Years 1803-4, Abstracted from the Journal of Abraham Pike, Riding Officer for the Collector of Customs.

'M' represents Mudeford (Haven) Quay.

'Q' represents Town Quay.

1803.

Month	From	Cargo Unloaded	At	Cargo Shipped	Destination
January	Portsmouth	Soap, Butter, Household furniture	M		
February	Poole	Stone	M	Malt, Barley	Portsmouth
	Chichester	Wheat	M		
	Chichester	Wheat	Q	Beer	Portsmouth
			M		
	Chichester	Wheat	Q	Beer, Malt	Portsmouth
			M		
March	Portsmouth	Claret, Brandy, Rum, Gnl. cargo	M	Beer, Malt, Barley	Portsmouth
	Lymington	Bricks, Tiles	Q	Wheat	Plymouth
			M		
	Chichester	Wheat	Q	Beer, Malt, Barley	Portsmouth

Month	Port	Cargo		Cargo	
April	Portsmouth	Coals	Q	Beer, Malt, Barley	Portsmouth
	Arundel	Wheat	Q	Beer, Malt, Flag rushes	Portsmouth
	Chichester	Wheat	M	Beer, Malt, Flagrushes	Portsmouth
			Q	Beer, Malt, Flagrushes, Timber	Portsmouth
			M		
May	Lymington	Coal	Q	Beer, Malt, Barley	Portsmouth
	Lymington	Coal	Q	Beer	Portsmouth
	Lymington	Coal	Q	Beer, Malt, Barley	Portsmouth
			M	Beer	Portsmouth
	Portsmouth	Coal	M	Malt	Portsmouth
	Portsmouth	Coal	Q		Portsmouth
			Q		
	Portland	Stone	Q		
			M		
	Poole	Stone	Q		
			M		
June	Chichester	Wheat	M	Rushes	Newport
	London	Beer, Porter	Q		
			M	Beech planks, Tiles	Lymington
			Q		
July	Chichester	Wheat	M	Biscuit	Plymouth
			M	Rushes	Portsmouth
			Q	Biscuit	Lymington
			M	Biscuit	Lymington
			M		

Month	Port	Cargo	Q/M	Cargo	Destination
August	Southampton	Coal, Slates	Q	Rushes	Portsmouth
			Q	Malt	Portsmouth
	Portsmouth	Coal	M	Biscuit	Plymouth
	Chichester	Wheat	M	Malt	Portsmouth
			Q	Wine, Oats, Barley, Wheat, Buckets	Shoreham
	Lymington	Coals, Tiles	Q	Biscuit	Plymouth
			M	Malt	Portsmouth
September	Portsmouth	Wheat	M	Wheat flour	London
	Chichester	Wheat, Household furniture	M		
	Poole	Stone	M	Malt	Portsmouth
	Chichester	Wheat	Q	Barley	Portsmouth
October	Portsmouth	Wine, Coals	Q	Rushes	Portsmouth
	Portsmouth	Coals, Butter, Soap	Q	Wheat flour, Malt	Portsmouth
			Q	Wheat flour, Beans, Malt, Potatoes	Portsmouth
			M	Tiles	Newhaven
			M	Wheat flour, Barley meal, Potatoes	Portsmouth
				Potatoes	